Economics After the Crisis

The Lionel Robbins Lectures

Peter Temin, *Lessons from the Great Depression* (1989)

Paul R. Krugman, *Exchange-Rate Instability* (1989)

Jeffrey Sachs, *Poland's Jump to the Market Economy* (1993)

Pedro Aspe, *Economic Transformation the Mexican Way* (1993)

Yegor Gaidar and Karl Otto Pohl, *Russian Reform/International Money* (1995)

Robert J. Barro, *Determinants of Economic Growth: A Cross-Country Empirical Study* (1997)

Alan S. Blinder, *Central Banking in Theory and Practice* (1998)

Ralph E. Gomory and William J. Baumol, *Global Trade and Conflicting National Interests* (2000)

Adair Turner, *Economics After the Crisis: Objectives and Means* (2012)

Economics After the Crisis

Objectives and Means

Adair Turner

The MIT Press
Cambridge, Massachusetts
London, England

© 2012 Massachusetts Institute of Technology

MIT Press books may be purchased at special quantity discounts for business or sales promotional use. For information, please email special_sales@mitpress.mit.edu or write to Special Sales Department, The MIT Press, 55 Hayward Street, Cambridge, MA 02142.

Set in Sabon by Graphic Composition, Inc. Printed and bound in the United States of America.

Library of Congress Cataloging-in-Publication Data

Turner, Adair.
Economics after the crisis : objectives and means / Adair Turner.
    p.   cm. — (The Lionel Robbins lectures)
Includes bibliographical references and index.
ISBN 978-0-262-01744-2 (hbk. : alk. paper)
1. Economic development. 2. Economic policy. 3. Free enterprise. 4. Economics. I. Title.
HD82.T86   2012
330—dc23

                                                                    2011040077

10   9   8   7   6   5   4   3   2   1

Contents

Foreword

Adair Turner is one of the most talented Britons of his generation. He is both an intellectual and a policy maker, and he has little time for those policy makers who are, as Keynes put it, simply "slaves of some defunct economist." In this book, based on his memorable 2010 Lionel Robbins Memorial Lectures, his purpose is no less than the rewriting of economics in the light of the current economic crisis.

The first issue is the goal of the economic system. Turner rejects the aim of maximizing the present value of the GDP. Instead he argues that much more importance should be attached to the quality of life, as people experience it. He reviews the evidence in full and concludes that a better quality of life depends on much more than economic growth. Among other things that matter are freedom and equality.

Where does the market fit into this? Turner is an expert on the financial markets. From his experience as Britain's chief regulator since 2008, he concludes that the crash of 2008 resulted from fundamental intellectual errors about the way markets work. The main error was the efficient-markets hypothesis, taken to imply that markets are socially efficient. If this were so, Turner asks, how could it be that credit default insurance traded at its lowest-ever price in June of 2007, months before the crisis began? Turner believes that much financial activity is an unproductive zero-sum game. To reduce the waste and the resulting economic instability, we need more regulation: much higher reserve requirements, more regulation of hot-money flows, and more grit in the wheels, as provided for example by the Tobin Tax. Completeness of markets and maximum liquidity are not, in his view, appropriate objectives.

Turner extends the argument to other issues, where again the principles of avoiding damage (loss aversion) should be given greater weight—to macroeconomics (where stability is crucial), to climate change (Turner chairs the UK Committee on Climate Change), to local choice (an essential bulwark against arbitrary damage from the center), and to population growth (lower population growth reduces the waste from positional competition).

As Turner points out, Robbins would not have agreed with everything he says. But they would have agreed on one thing: that standard received economic theory has clear limitations and cannot on its own tell us what we should do.

Richard Layard

Introduction

The capitalist system has suffered a great crisis. And when the crisis intensified dramatically in the autumn of 2008, many commentators emphasized its wide-ranging nature. The prospects for the economy were discussed in apocalyptic terms—a new Great Depression threatened. But there was also talk of a crisis in political legitimacy and a likely paradigm shift in political economy: an end to the era of unfettered, finance-driven Anglo-Saxon capitalism, and an end to the era of greed. Many thought that a shift to left-wing politics and to more redistribution was likely, and that new ideas and policies as radical as those of the New Deal would be proposed and implemented. Some believed that what had failed was not just a financial system, and a way of regulating that financial system, but a set of economic theories, and that we should now reject the simplicities of neoliberal and neoclassical economics, reject overly mathematical economics, and return to the insights of the past. Robert Skidelsky, in a book both brilliant and brilliantly timed, wrote of "the return of the master," meaning John Maynard Keynes.[1]

Three years on, how do those forecasts of apocalyptical results and radical change look?

The good news is that we have not suffered a Great Depression remotely comparable to that of 1929–1933. Recovery has been painfully slow, and new financial stresses have emerged that could lead to further setbacks. But the warnings of economic apocalypse turn out to have been overstated. This is because the policy responses were better than in 1929–1933. Even in October of 2008, there were good reasons to believe that our economic understanding—deriving from the experience of 1929–1933—gave us the macroeconomic tools we needed to prevent disaster.

The developments in political economy have been complex. In general, left-wing parties have not gained from this crisis of capitalism. In the United Kingdom, in 2010, a coalition of moderate free-marketers took over from an incumbent party of the left that had itself largely embraced market ideology and language. In the United States, Barack Obama's victory in the 2008 presidential election raised expectations of major change, but there has been no shift in the balance of American public opinion away from free-market capitalism remotely comparable to that which accompanied Franklin D. Roosevelt's changes in the 1930s. Bankers may have been vilified, but there has been no fundamental rejection of free-market assumptions in Europe or in the United States.

In the discipline of economics, there have been major debates about appropriate macroeconomic policy and about economic theory. In April of 2010, the inaugural meeting of the Institute for New Economic Thinking, held at Cambridge University, brought together numerous opponents of recently dominant conventional wisdoms. But whether there will be any lasting change in the practice of academic economics remains unclear.

So it is at least possible that the great crash of 2008–2009, apparently so earth-changing at the time, may, in the long sweep of history, prove a far less radical turning point than either the crisis of free-market capitalism in the early 1930s, and the shift to the left that it produced, or the crisis of managed capitalism in the 1960s and the 1970s, and the shift to the right that it produced.

Should the crash of 2008 prompt a serious re-evaluation of economic and political assumptions and of economic theory? Or is the correct response simply careful management of the major macroeconomic challenges we face as we seek to recover from a recession, alongside major reform of financial regulation to prevent another crisis—but with overall assumptions about the objectives and the means of market economics continuing much as before?

My answer will be that the crisis *should* prompt us to challenge fundamental assumptions and to raise issues that go beyond those directly raised by the impact of the crisis itself. For I believe that the faults of theory and policy that led to the crisis in the financial system were elements of a wider set of simplistic beliefs about the objectives and means of economic activity that dominated policy thinking for several decades before 2008: that maximizing economic growth was the clear objective and that markets were the universally applicable means of achieving it. We need to move beyond those beliefs if we are not only to build a more stable financial system for the future but also to address more fundamental issues about how rich developed countries achieve progress in human welfare, or at least avoid setbacks to it.

This book is therefore intended as a rejection of a dominant conventional wisdom, but not as a rejection of market economics or of liberal capitalism. Indeed, I will suggest that we should return to justifications of economic freedom that are more fundamental than those put forward in the recent dominant conventional wisdom, but which, because they are political, necessarily involve us in debates about choices and tradeoffs. And I will argue that economics, to be most useful, must be closely connected to a wider discipline of political economy—a philosophical, empirical, historical, and ethical discipline, as well as a rigorously mathematical one.

I will develop a detailed and extensive argument to support these propositions. But to make it easy to follow, let me give a brief overview:

• Over the course of several decades before the crisis, there had developed a dominant political discourse about economic objectives and a conventional wisdom about the means with which to pursue them. Three assumptions lay at the heart of this thinking:

The crucial objective of successful policy is more rapid growth in measured prosperity (that is, in per capita GDP). Enhanced national competitiveness was seen as a measure of a government's competence. "It's the economy, stupid," said both Bill Clinton and Tony Blair.

The primary way to deliver growth is by creating freer markets—freeing entrepreneurs from red tape, unleashing incentives through lighter income taxes and capital-gains taxes, extending markets by means of privatization and liberalization. In particular, freer and more complete financial markets drive economic growth by enabling a more efficient allocation of capital.

A significant degree of inequality is both the inevitable consequence of and necessary to the operation of free markets, and that increased inequality is acceptable because and to the extent that it helps deliver superior growth.

In the 30 years or so before the crisis, this package of ideas—which I will label "the instrumental conventional wisdom"—became increasingly dominant across the political spectrum. But all three of these assumptions are now challenged, to different degrees, by facts and by more thoughtful reflections on theory:

• It is not clear that long-term economic growth should be the overriding objective of policy in rich developed countries, since it is not clear that it necessarily delivers increased human welfare, or happiness, or utility, or whatever it is that should be our ultimate goal. (Short-to-medium-term growth from today's starting point—from the depths of recession—is, in contrast, undoubtedly very important, and in chapter 3 I will seek to explain why that can be true even though long-term growth maximization should not be the overriding objective.[2])

• One reason among many why economic growth may not deliver increased well-being is that inequality probably matters quite a lot to human happiness, and problems created by inequality cannot be swept away by growth.

• Free markets are not a universally applicable means of achieving faster growth. Although free markets work very well in some areas of economic activity (in the restaurant industry, for instance), in other areas (finance in particular) problems of market failure are endemic and cannot be fixed by simply making markets still freer and more transparent.

In this book I will explore these three challenges to the dominant political ideology and the underpinning economic theory of the last 30 years.

In chapter 1, I will consider objectives—why more rapid growth should not be the overriding objective for rich developed countries, and whether and how much inequality should concern us.

In chapter 2, I will turn to the role of markets, and in particular financial markets, as means by which to pursue objectives. I will argue that the pre-crisis confidence in free financial markets was profoundly misplaced.

In chapter 3, I will consider where my conclusions leave the case for economic freedom, what implications might follow in specific areas of public policy (including financial regulation, climate change, demography, local government), and our attitude toward income inequality. I will also consider what implications follow for the discipline of economics, relating my conclusions to those reached in 1932 by Lionel Robbins, who, in a brilliant essay titled *On the Nature and Significance of Economic Science*,[3] set out a strong point of view on what the subject matter of economics should be, drawing a distinction between the objectives and the means of economic activity and clearly delineating economics from politics, psychology, and philosophy.[4] My conclusions may seem different, agreeing with Keynes, who argued that "as against Robbins, economics is essentially a moral science." But a careful reading of Robbins's essay suggests that the difference is less fundamental than it first appears, and that if subsequent economists and users of economics had heeded Robbins's warnings about the limitations of economics narrowly defined they would have been more wary of the simplicities of the instrumental conventional wisdom.

1
Economic Gtowth, Human Welfare, and Inequality

Let us begin with the objectives of economic activity and policy.

In the second half of the twentieth century, the idea became increasingly dominant that attaining a superior gtowth rate and thus increased prosperity should be the central objective of public policy.

Other issues—culture, morals, religion, national identity—were not entirely absent, but, in contrast with nineteenth-century or early-twentieth-century politics, the main electoral battlegtound was often the issue of which political pafty would best deliver material prosperity. Harold Macmillan's election campaign in 1959 was built on the assertion "We've never had it so good." In the 1960s, Harold Wilson's Labour government was determined to boost the UK's rate of gtowth to that being achieved in Continental Europe. Margaret Thatcher's promise was essentially that, after some tough medicine, prosperity would gtow faster under the Conservatives than under Labour.

The shared assumption across the political spectrum was that economic gtowth—both in GDP and in per capita GDP—would result directly in increasing well-being, welfare, happiness, contentment, or whatever word we use, and therefore would lead to political success for the party best able to deliver it. The debate was essentially about what policies would achieve that end, how large a role markets should play in delivering prosperity, and what level of inequality was required to ensure economic success and was acceptable as a by-product.

The conservative narrative, asserted with increasing confidence toward the end of the century, was that free markets were the best way to deliver prosperity, and that significant inequality was acceptable—indeed required—because it gave entrepreneurs, executives, and ordinary workers incentives that would ensure innovation, competitive success in global markets, high productivity growth, and thus increasing prosperity. Whereas in the nineteenth century conservatives defended inequality and property rights as elements of a natural order, in the late twentieth century conservative parties tended to advance an instrumental justification of both markets and inequality: that flexible markets and low taxes on the rich were good because they would make the average citizen richer. As a result, parties of the right (to different degrees in different countries) tended to be defined less by the classic parameters of conservatism—nation, social order, religion, received morals and culture—than in the past, becoming instead parties of liberal economic ideology.

Meanwhile, parties of the left had to decide how much of this narrative they accepted and how much of it was compatible with egalitarian instincts. Reactions differed by country and between parties with strong Marxist traditions and those more willing to accept the amelioration of workers' conditions within capitalism as an acceptable objective rather than as either a stepping stone or an impediment to revolutionary change. But the direction of change everywhere was toward at least a partial acceptance, and in some countries a positive embrace, of liberal economic ideology. The role of social-democratic parties was to smooth the rough distributional edges of the market economy, but three assumptions spread across the political spectrum: that markets helped to create growth in GDP, that growth in GDP led to improved social well-being and individual welfare, and that significant inequality was acceptable because and to the extent that it helped deliver enterprise, competitive success, productivity growth, and increasing per capita GDP.

But even as that consensus has grown, it has become increasingly unclear whether there is a strong link between average per capita GDP and people's average happiness or welfare once the levels of average income already attained in rich developed countries have been reached. And that has profound implications for how we should think about the objectives of economic policy and about the validity of what I have labeled the instrumental justification of markets and inequality.

Of course, any discussion of the relationship between income and happiness raises questions about whether happiness should be the objective and, if so, whether happiness can be measured. On these two issues I am somewhat more skeptical about the precision of what we can assert than are Richard Layard and some other economists.[1] On the first, the problems

of aggregation and of possible competing objectives—justice, virtue, freedom—seem to me significant. Suppose that people are "happy" under a
dictatorial regime. Would we accept that as a good result? Or suppose
that 99.9 percent are made ecstatically happy by the human sacrifice of a
minute minority. Would we say that was OK? And is happiness the same
as welfare? If it isn't, precisely how does it differ? And when we use surveys of self-perceived happiness in different time periods and in different
countries, how certain are we that there aren't important differences in
how people answer those questions?

These are all non-trivial problems, but I don't believe they are fatal to
the limited proposition I will assert, which is not that we can define a gross
national happiness index as the objective and measure our achievement of
it, but simply a negative hypothesis with two components:

• We have no good reason for believing that additional growth in average
income, as measured by national income accounts, will necessarily and
limitlessly deliver increased happiness, well-being, welfare, or whatever
we define as the objective.[2]

• There are fairly strong grounds for believing that rich developed countries are now in the zone where further increases in average income are of
uncertain and in some respects diminishing importance.

With all due caveats about difficulties of definition and measurement, I
will argue that a combination of empirical evidence, *a priori* logic, and
common-sense observation of human nature strongly supports those
conclusions.

1.1   Empirical Evidence: Contesting Claims

The empirical evidence is contested. In 1995 Richard Easterlin challenged
the axiomatic assumption that increasing income necessarily and limitlessly increases human satisfaction, arguing that beyond some level of average per capita income no such relationship exists.[3] Bruno Frey and Alois
Stutzer's work has appeared to confirm Easterlin's proposition.[4] Richard
Layard's book *Happiness* accepted the lack of correlation between happiness and average income, beyond some level of income, as an established
fact. But the work of Justin Wolfers and Angus Deaton (among others)
has challenged this.

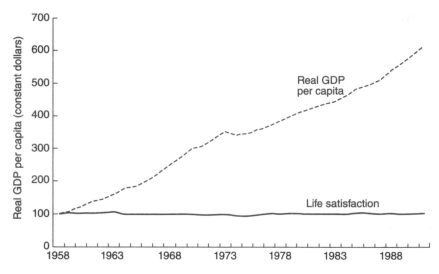

Figure 1.1
Satisfaction with life and growth of income in Japan. Source: Penn World Tables and World Database of Happiness, as referenced in Bruno Frey and Alois Stutzer, *Happiness and Economics* (Princeton University Press, 2002).

The empirical case against the value of growth is that surveys of self-assessed "life satisfaction" or "happiness" from several rich developed countries with different cultural characteristics suggest that over the last 40 to 50 years there has been no improvement, despite very significant increases in per capita GDP. Figures 1.1 and 1.2 show the results for Japan and the United States. Meanwhile, cross-country comparisons, such as those in figure 1.3, suggested that there was a fairly strong relationship between income and self-perceived happiness or "contentment with life" for per capita incomes up to about $15,000 or $20,000, but that further increments in average income make little difference.[5] In stylized form, the empirical evidence has therefore seemed consistent with the pattern shown in figure 1.4—a pattern applicable in a time-series sense as well as in a cross-sectional sense: it seems that countries experience major increases in human welfare and self-perceived contentment as their income grows from low levels to about the equivalent of $20,000 per year, but beyond that level measured income continues to increase without significant aggregate welfare benefit.

The transition from very low income levels to those seen in rich developed countries today is, of course, a great and historically unique

Figure 1.2
Happiness and per capita income in the United States. Source: World Database of Happiness, U.S. Department of Commerce Bureau of Economic Analysis, and U.S. Census Bureau, as referenced in Frey and Stutzer, *Happiness and Economics*.

achievement of the last 200 years. (See table 1.1.) For the whole of human history until about 1000 AD, average standards of living showed no sustained tendency to increase. Though any quantification is highly uncertain, Angus Maddison's estimate that in most parts of the world per capita GDP was about $400 per capita still probably captures the essence of reality.[6] Quality of diet and life expectancy varied with the vagaries of disease, war, and climate. Fluctuations in political regimes and culture produced changes in the level of sophistication of elite groups, reflected in their art, their household possessions, and their architecture. But the modern assumption and reality that each century—indeed each decade—would bring new technologies, new products, increased income, and significant changes in lifestyle were entirely absent in the pre-modern world.

The change that then occurred, first in Western Europe and then elsewhere, glacially from 1000 to 1500, very gradually from 1500 to 1800,

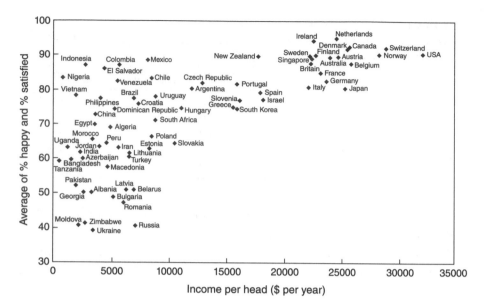

Figure 1.3
Comparison of income and happiness in various countries. Source: World Values Survey, as referenced in Richard Layard, *Happiness* (Penguin, 2005).

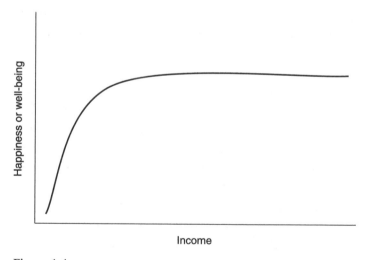

Figure 1.4
Possible stylized pattern of average income and happiness or well-being.

Table 1.1
Average per capita GDP in 1990 dollars. Source: Angus Maddison, *The World Economy: A Millennial Perspective* (OECD, 2006).

	1000	1500	1870	1998
Western Europe	400	775	1200	18000
Western offshoots	400	400	1200	26000
Japan	420	500	670	20000
Asia (excluding Japan)	450	570	575	3000
Africa	400	400	400	1400

and then explosively over the last two centuries, was the second great transformation in human economic history, equivalent in impact to the development of agriculture from the eighth millennium BC on, though far more sudden.[7]

The empirical evidence presented by Richard Easterlin, Richard Layard, Bruno Frey, and Alois Stutzer appears to illustrate that the early stages of this transition were strongly positive for human well-being, but that beyond some level of income there is a flattening of the relationship between income and well-being. (See figure 1.5.) And it seems intuitively obvious that increasing productivity and income from pre-modern levels to those enjoyed by rich developed countries should have had a major effect on human well-being.

That increase has raised life expectancy, has freed people from the drudgery of manual labor, has abolished (in most societies) such primary detriments to human happiness as hunger, inadequate clothing, and inadequate housing, and has delivered a cornucopia of material goods and services that delight and stimulate us. It is an extraordinary achievement. And as best we can tell, it has increased human happiness and self-perceived contentment.

I will therefore accept it as given that further growth is still a priority for human welfare in the many societies that have not yet completed this transition—a high priority for China, still at an early stage in the transformation, and even more so for what Paul Collier has called "The Bottom Billion"[8]—the many people, particularly in certain African countries, who have yet to enjoy much economic progress at all. However, my subject here is not how to achieve an economic growth transformation in the bottom billion, important though that is, but what we can say about the

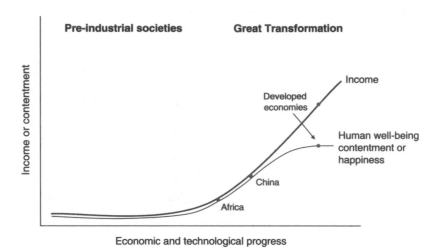

Figure 1.5
Possible stylized pattern of income, contentment, and economic and technological progress.

objectives of economic activity and economic policy once countries have achieved the great transformation.

Figures 1.1–1.3 imply that increasing average per capita GDP has no ability to produce increases in human well-being in countries that have achieved the transformation.

That conclusion is, however, strongly contested by some researchers. Daniel Sacks, Betsey Stevenson, and Justin Wolfers, for instance, argue in a recent paper that both cross-country and time-series data illustrate continuing increases in human satisfaction or happiness even as incomes rise above what other researchers have identified as possible points of inflection.[9] Plotting life satisfaction versus real per capita GDP with a log scale for per capita GDP (figure 1.6), they argue that the evidence is consistent with the interpretation that doubling average annual income from $16,000 to $32,000 is as important to life satisfaction as increasing it from $1,000 to $2,000, and that the difficulty previous researchers have had observing this fact may have been attributable to the fact that differences between the per capita incomes of rich developed countries are, in proportional terms, extremely slight. Similarly, they argue that time-series data do suggest a positive upward slope of average life satisfaction, at both high and low income levels, as average income rises.

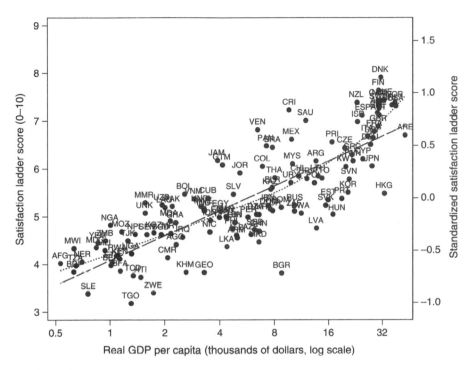

Figure 1.6
Life satisfaction and real per capita GDP. Source: Daniel W. Sacks, Betsy Stevenson, and Justin Wolfers, Subjective Well-Being, Income, Economic Development and Growth, NBER working paper 16441, 2010.

This counter-evidence casts some doubt on previous assertions that the relationship between average income and average life satisfaction flattens out entirely above a certain income level. And, as I will argue later in this chapter and in chapter 3, the proposal that there might be *no* net life-satisfaction benefit from increasing absolute income beyond some threshold has always seemed counter-intuitive.[10] For instance, since average income growth is capable of delivering improvements in health and in life expectancy (and reductions in the incidence of early death), and since evidence has always suggested that better health is strongly correlated with perceived well-being, it would be surprising if this potential positive effect were not achieved and apparent.

But the new evidence leaves intact the finding that the relationship between average income and human well-being is, at least for rich developed countries, uncertain and complex. It is, for instance, noticeable in

Sacks, Stevenson, and Wolfers's analysis that long-term changes in average income appear to have much less of an effect than changes over shorter time periods. This is consistent with the hypothesis that individuals adjust to new circumstances and that their aspirations change over time, so that well-being gains from increased income eventually dissipate.[11] And the time-series findings drawn from the Eurobarometer survey (which ought to provide some of the best empirical evidence, since they are based on consistent questions and since they compare culturally similar countries) suggest a complex and uncertain relationship between average income and life satisfaction. The overall correlation of decadal changes in life satisfaction (shown on the vertical axis of figure 1.7) to per capita GDP (shown on the horizontal axis) is weak. And the comparisons of the results for different countries are not at all consistent with the assumptions of the instrumental conventional wisdom. The correlation suggests, for instance,

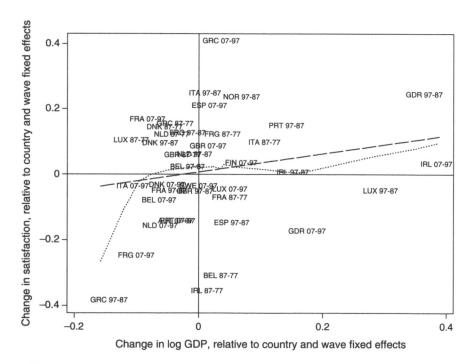

Figure 1.7
Decadal differences in life satisfaction and log GDP. Source: Sacks, Stevenson, and Wolfers, Subjective Well-Being, Income, Economic Development and Growth, NBER working paper 16441, 2010.

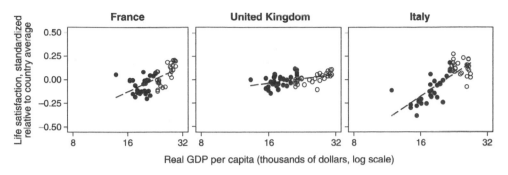

Figure 1.8
Changes in life satisfaction and economic growth in Europe.

that France and Italy have been much more successful than the United Kingdom at turning growth in per capita GDP into increased life satisfaction. (See figure 1.8.) If these figures are truly telling us what they appear to be telling us, a British government that wished to ensure increasing life satisfaction for its citizens would devote very little attention to increasing per capita GDP growth, and most of its attention to understanding what it is about the pattern of growth being achieved in France and Italy that appears to be producing more significant increases in life satisfaction.

Thus, while we should be careful before leaping from the assumption that growth necessarily drives happiness to its opposite—i.e., Richard Easterlin's apparent certainty that there is no relationship between average income and average life satisfaction above a certain level—the evidence is certainly compatible with the conclusion that there are many drivers of life satisfaction other than measured income growth, and that the precise pattern of growth matters at least as much as its absolute level. We certainly do not have good reason for believing that further growth in measured per capita GDP will *necessarily* deliver further significant increases in human contentment.

1.2   Explanations for the Disconnection between Average Income and Happiness

Why might a breakdown occur in the relationship between average income growth and human contentment? There are several easily identifiable reasons. Indeed, given the factors that could support Richard Easterlin's and

Richard Layard's assertions, it is difficult to see how economic growth could be expected to deliver increments in human contentment limitlessly, for both the very process of becoming rich and the changing nature of what a rich economy produces and consumes are likely to undermine the logical linkages between average income and average utility.

One major change that has occurred as we have become richer has been the transition from a primarily industrial economy to a service-dominated economy in which an increasing proportion of total consumption is devoted to services rather than to goods. But that transition in itself, and the distinction between material goods and immaterial services, is not fundamental to the issues I am discussing here. Indeed, Lionel Robbins made that point in his 1932 lecture.[12] If increments to happiness are produced by increased measured prosperity, happiness is as likely to be produced by more restaurant meals and more gardeners as by more washing machines and more cars.

The most obvious reason why increasing income may not deliver significant increases in contentment is the simple theory of satiation—of declining marginal benefits. One winter coat keeps you warm; two winter coats don't keep you warmer, but give you a second-order benefit of fashion and style. This common-sense assumption about human preferences is expressed in the formal economic concept of diminishing marginal utility (figure 1.9). But although this concept might help explain a steadily weaker relationship between income and increased contentment, it could not explain the complete disappearance of the relationship.

Indeed, it can be argued that the formal economic concept of diminishing marginal utility doesn't even necessarily explain declining *aggregate* marginal utility with respect to all income and all consumption. Strictly applied, the concept of declining marginal utility relates to the consumption of a particular good, and determines the price of that particular good, given the alternative of consuming other goods.[13] In a continually creative economy, there could be many products the consumption of which is approaching satiation, but a continual flow of new products and services such that each individual's consumption is still on the steep early section of the curve (figure 1.10). An assumption of potential aggregate declining utility can still be reasonable, given a hierarchy of human needs—an iPad must be less important to human contentment than freedom from hunger. But declining marginal utility as a result of increasing satiation

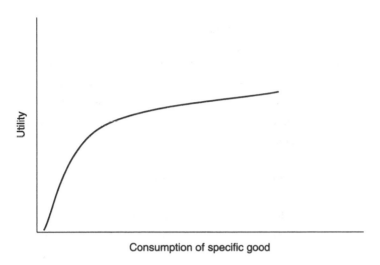

Figure 1.9
Diminishing marginal utility.

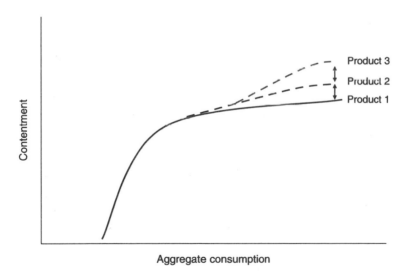

Figure 1.10
Contentment and aggregate consumption: the effect of new products and services.

would still be an inadequate explanation of a *complete* disappearance of any link between income and contentment.

The flattening of the aggregate curve suggested by some empirical evidence becomes more understandable, however, if we consider three ways in which the nature of consumption and its relationship to human well-being is in itself changed by the very fact of rising income:

• The richer people become, the more they choose to devote their income to buying goods delineated by style, fashion, and brand, so as to signal that they are in with or ahead of the crowd. But the higher other people's income becomes, the wider the range of goods and services over which this relative-status competition occurs. There has, for instance, been significant growth in families' expenditures on children, driven in part by the desire to ensure that one's child doesn't feel deprived of relative status as a result of lacking the latest fashionable toy, electronic gadget, or item of branded clothing. There is no evidence that this has made childhood a happier, more pleasant experience; indeed, some would argue that it has done the inverse. Whether or not relative-status competition may have a negative effect, increased expenditures on relative-status goods, made possible by higher income, are very unlikely to drive a sustained increase in contentment. And that must also be true of the large slice of income expended on branded and fashion goods for adults.

• In addition, as people get richer, they devote a higher percentage of their income to competing for the enjoyment of locationally specific amenities that are inherently in short supply, and each person's ability to afford those amenities is determined by relative income, not by absolute income. To be able to stay at the hotel on the beach rather than at one a mile away, or at the hotel on the ski slope rather than at one down the valley, what matters is not your absolute income, but your income relative to everyone else, and an increase in average per capita GDP can make no difference to that. And although skiing and beach hotels may seem to be minor issues, competition for housing amenities is clearly not minor. As we get richer, we devote an increasing percentage of our income to competing to buy houses in more pleasant places, and our ability to win in that competition is driven entirely by relative income, not absolute income.

• Increases in aggregate income can produce environmental externalities that are detrimental to human well-being. Some of these effects can be overcome through the achievements of growth itself—that is, through improvements in technology. For example, local air quality has improved steadily in most rich countries over the last 30 years. But some externality effects are inherently difficult to deal with. (I will address climate change in chapter 3.) And important congestion effects are almost inherent in the very process of getting richer. As we get richer, more people can afford skiing, beach, or countryside holidays, and the ski slope, the beach, and the countryside get more crowded, which degrades the experiences people seek to enjoy. Driving a car along country roads in 1950s Britain—for the minority that could then afford it—was a more pleasant experience than doing so today, simply because one was much less likely to be driving bumper to bumper. And a large proportion of the car advertisements on British television today—apparently shot on rural roads in Scotland or Scandinavia at 4 o'clock on a summer morning—are almost bound to produce frustration, since they entice you to buy an experience—driving along an open road—that can almost never be delivered. In many ways, therefore, as we get richer, if we don't manage the process very carefully, increasing wealth degrades the very benefits it seems to make more generally available.

Each of these three factors helps to explain why, beyond some income level, further average income growth is not certain to deliver significant sustained increases in contentment. And each has specific characteristics and effects.

The first factor is relevant only if relative status, as evidenced by consumption of fashion or branded goods or by being an early adopter of the latest gadget, is an end in itself. And it is therefore a factor from which some people could escape: if you don't care what label your clothes bear, it doesn't apply. But for many people it does apply.

The second factor, however, makes relative income a crucial driver of absolute standard of living, even for those not concerned with relative status. Even if you are unmoved by relative status per se, and perfectly happy if everyone else has a house as nice as yours, if the supply of pleasant houses is restricted then you have to seek to win in the relative-income competition. And the closer we come to satiation of basic needs, the higher the percentage of our income we devote to such competition.

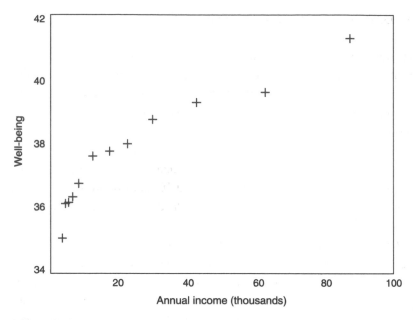

Figure 1.11
Income and well-being in the United States, 1981–1984). Happiness is measured on a scale from 0 (extremely unhappy) to 55 (extremely happy). Points represent averages for income categories from a sample of 4,942 individuals. Source: Ed Diener et al., "The Relationship between Income and Subjective Well-Being: Relative or Absolute?" *Social Indicators Research* 28, no. 3 (1993): 195–223.

The third factor, meanwhile, means that in some ways the total available utility for which we compete is itself diminished by the very fact of increased aggregate income.

So these are three distinct factors, but they have a common implication. It is that the implicit assumption of any simply presented marginal-utility curve—that my utility is a function of my income alone—is clearly wrong. My utility is clearly also a function of other people's income and of my income relative to that of others. And together the first two factors mean that the empirical finding that richer people in any one country are on average happier than poorer people (figure 1.11) is both what we would expect and entirely compatible with a finding that, when considered on a time-series basis, an increase in *average* income doesn't certainly and strongly translate into an increase in *average* contentment.[14]

1.3   Distributive and Creative Activities

As I have just discussed, the changing pattern of consumption, a direct result of increasing income, itself changes the logically expected relationship between income and human contentment. It seems likely, in addition, that important and subtle changes in the pattern of production activity—of how people earn income—are also at work.

A crucial distinction here is between what Roger Bootle, in his recent book *The Trouble with Markets*,[15] labels "creative" and purely "distributive" activities—a distinction close to what William Baumol highlighted in his delineation of "Entrepreneurship: Productive, Unproductive and Destructive."[16]

That distinction has always been present in market economies, and indeed in all human societies. The clever lawyer who wins a case for his client achieves a redistribution of money from the opposing client but doesn't create greater social value. The financial trader who bets well makes money at the expense of the one who bets badly. Indeed, though it may be possible to describe some jobs as, in Bootle's terms, almost entirely and directly "creative" (e.g., a doctor directly providing the value of better health), the majority of jobs in a developed market economy are partly distributive and partly creative, though often creative in indirect ways. The salesman who gains an order for company A is involved in an activity whose first-order effect is distributive, but it may be indirectly creative if company A is more efficient than company B, so that its growth relative to company B will help make the economy more productive.[17,18] The market economy creates growth not because every person is continually involved in activities that, in classic income-accounting terms, "create value," but because on average competition between individuals and firms, many of whose day-to-day activities are in their direct effects purely distributive, tends over time to deliver improvements in productive efficiency and to deliver new products that consumers value.

So the existence of "distributive" activity is not new. Bootle, however, suggests that "the more developed a society becomes . . . the more it is at risk of behavior that merely redistributes rather than creates." And there are certainly many ways in which we could expect purely distributive activities to become more prevalent as average income increases:

• Financial services (particularly wholesale trading activities) include a large share of highly remunerated activities that are purely distributive in their indirect effects—and the share of financial services in our economy has grown.

• Richer societies tend to be more litigious societies. Litigation is essentially a zero-sum distributive activity, and lawyers are highly paid.

• In rich societies, consumers are able to devote a significant slice of income to buying goods solely because they bear a brand—for example, celebrity A's perfume versus celebrity B's. But brand competition of this sort is essentially distributive rather than value-added. It is therefore distinct in its economic function from the early development of branding, which performed an important function in enabling products of consistent quality to dominate over the multiplicity of lower-quality and sometimes dangerous products.

I do not know how far such distributive activities—in marketing and public relations, in much of financial services, in legal services—have increased as a percentage of the total economy; it would be an interesting subject for research. But I regard Bootle's hypothesis that they will tend to become more extensive as society gets richer as reasonable. It has two important implications:

• The richer we get, as measured by per capita GDP, the more arbitrary and uncertain some of the conventions required to calculate GDP become.[19] In principle, measures of per capita GDP exclude purely distributive activities (for example, the gains of one poker player at the expense of others); in practice, however, their ability to do so is highly imperfect. In particular, the ability of national income accounts to distinguish within financial services between activities that are meaningfully value-creative and activities that are essentially distributive rent extraction is far from perfect (an issue explored by Andrew Haldane and others in their chapter in the recent London School of Economics report *The Future of Finance*).[20]

• For reasons I will explore below, it is noticeable that many of the most highly paid and presumably most highly skilled people earn their living from essentially distributive activities in which the application of still higher skills must simply increase the intensity of distributional competition rather than deliver benefits that are at all likely to deliver sustained improvements in average contentment. If over a period of time the intensity of divorce litigation increases, and the income of divorce lawyers increases, and if as a result more highly skilled people seek to become divorce lawyers, we should not expect society to gain from that reallocation of skilled human resources, even though the output of divorce lawyers shows up in GDP calculations as much as that of highly skilled doctors.

1.4   Increasing Inequality and Its Implications

An increasingly rich economy is therefore likely to be one in which both more of consumption and more of productive activities are devoted to zero-sum and distributive competition. It is also one in which relative income and status are crucial to an individual's sense of well-being and in which relative skill is crucial to success in the competition for higher income. In view of these changes, it should not surprise us that the relationship between income growth and self-perceived well-being is uncertain in rich developed societies—particularly since in rich developed countries, with relative income becoming more important, inequality has tended to increase. This increase in inequality has two dimensions. First, there is a tendency, most prominent in Anglo-Saxon countries and especially in the United States, for the bottom of the income distribution to fall further behind the median. Second, there is a very strong tendency, most extreme in the United States but also pronounced in the United Kingdom and significant throughout the developed world, for the top to pull away from the middle and for the very rich to pull away from the moderately rich. Over the last 30 years, increases in the income of the top decile have far exceeded those of the median, the top percentile has done better than the rest of the top decile, and the top 0.1 percent of the population has pulled far away from the rest of the top 1 percent.

The decline in the relative position of the poorest has been analyzed extensively. The most likely explanation is a number of interlocking primary and secondary causes. One of the primary causes is technology, which, by reducing the need for unskilled or semi-skilled manual labor, has reduced the relative marginal product of relatively less skilled people. Two other causes are globalization and more mobile factors of production—more open trade, freer movement of capital, and freer movement of people (for instance, the end, in the 1960s and the 1970s, of the restrictions on immigration into the United States put in place in the 1920s). Each of these forms of easier factor movement would be predicted by economic theory to produce aggregate income benefits but also to produce distributional effects—that is, an increase in the average income level of people in richer countries but a decline in the relative income of the less skilled. In addition to these primary effects, however, the erosion of trade unions' power and of collective bargaining structures, itself partly an endogenous consequence of greater openness to trade and capital movements, has certainly played a role.

Increasing inequality at the top of the income and wealth distribution of society has been less extensively analyzed. However, it seems likely that it is driven, at least in part, by the changes in the nature of consumption and production that occur naturally as societies become richer on average. Even while increasing average income makes relative income more important to human contentment, it may also unleash tendencies that, unless counteracted, will automatically tend toward increasing income dispersion.

At least four interlocking forces combine to make increasing inequality at the top an almost inevitable consequence of rising average prosperity. Three are in some sense inherent, driven by changes in the underlying equilibrium value of private marginal product; the fourth is a social phenomenon that is in part exogenous but in part an endogenous consequence of the first three.

• One striking development at the top of the distribution is increasing returns to stardom or celebrity achieved through high sporting or artistic skill. Stanley Matthews, one of the football greats of 1950s Britain, earned an adequate middle-class living; David Beckham is among the super-rich. As a novelist, C. S. Lewis made adequate money; J. K. Rowling became a billionaire. Technology and globalization are among the forces at work here: television and the Internet made David Beckham and Harry Potter global brands.[21] But rising average income is also important. As people's income rises, they devote more of it to providing themselves or their children with the latest branded merchandise, without which relative status is lost. And buying that merchandise puts more money in the hands of celebrities. One reason why David Beckham is far richer than Stanley Matthews is that the average income of his fans is high enough to allow significant discretionary expenditures both on more expensive tickets and on goods that bear his brand or which he endorses. And although superstars are few, once the minor stars, the passing celebrities, the agents, the lawyers, the PR firms, and the executives of the media channels are included, and the party organizers, and the providers of luxury goods, and up-market hoteliers and restaurateurs, we have a phenomenon that helps to accelerate income growth throughout the top income decile, as well as at the pinnacle of enormous wealth. As Lionel Robbins perceptively noted in 1932, "a substantial proportion of the high incomes of the rich is due to the existence of other rich people."[22]

• In parallel, meanwhile, the changing nature of consumption, and its increasing devotion to goods or services that are not essential in the hierarchy of human needs but nice to have, demand for which is driven by fashion or caprice, means that in some areas of economic activity highly talented individuals can make their companies successful more rapidly and in a highly measurable way. A talented retailer with a flair for store design and ambience, for range selection, and for marketing can make a huge difference to a retail chain's success quite quickly, whereas a talented manufacturing manager can do so only over many years, as research and development or improvements in manufacturing efficiency slowly reach fruition. And the shorter the time period over which results are achieved, and the more easily those results seem to be identifiable with the individual rather than the team, so the more likely they are to be reflected in individual remuneration. The higher the percentage of our consumption devoted to goods and services for which style, ambience, and brand matter, the higher may be the naturally arising inequality at the top of the distribution.

• This phenomenon of highly measurable and immediate economic impact is particularly present in some of the activities that are most clearly—in Roger Bootle's terms—distributive rather than creative. The successful divorce lawyer redistributes income in favor of his or her client and away from the other lawyer's client, and the lawyer's success in doing so is immediately apparent in a way that the success of a research scientist working alongside many others on a new drug that will reach patients many years hence is not. Top lawyers therefore typically earn more than top scientists; and the more litigious a society is, in either personal or commercial cases, the larger the number of high-earning lawyers will be. The reason why successful financial traders are paid so much is that their distributive economic impact—the extent to which they have made their firms richer at the expense of others—appears to be very large and immediately measurable. Sometimes, of course, that is because success this year is at the expense of a trail of toxic liabilities in the future, and financial regulators are trying to fix that problem by demanding bonus deferral and claw-back arrangements. But even when we regulators have done that, I suspect, we will still see financial traders paid highly for activities that are, at least in part, distributive rather than creative. As a result, a large financial-services sector within the economy will tend to result in a wide income disparity between the top few percentiles and the median of the distribution.

• The three forces already mentioned help to change attitudes, and that in itself unleashes further change. If the worlds of celebrity, fashion, and media generate very high pay, and if there are more highly paid corporate lawyers and investment bankers than there once were, and if there are some businesses (e.g., fashion retailing) in which a star CEO can make a big difference and get highly rewarded, then the sense among highly paid people of what is normal and justifiable shifts.[23] In addition, the income they need in order to afford houses in the best part of town increases because the prices of those houses are set by the average income of the rest of the income elite. If we then add the impact of a partly global market in executive talent, and the activities of remuneration consultants with their comparisons between this CEO and that, and the role that relative-status competition plays in the motivations of high talented people, we have the ingredients for the relentless rise in the relative income of not just the few top stars but the top 1 percent of the population that we have seen over the last 30 years.

What the balance is between these four forces, and in particular between those that are in a sense inherent and those that reflect changing social attitudes and business practices, I do not know. But I think it is clear that a complex combination of narrowly economic and wider social factors, with the latter somewhat driven by the former, has produced a significant increase in inequality at the top of the income distribution. In the dominant narrative of the last 30 years, this increase was justified because and to the extent that it had made the economy more efficient, more competitive, and thus faster growing. But there is no clear evidence that it had that supposedly beneficial effect, nor is it clear whether higher measured growth, if achieved, implies rising average well-being.

Thus, we have increases in inequality that seem likely to be, in part, inherent consequences of the very fact that we are getting richer, rather than themselves drivers of increased prosperity. Does this matter? If it does, can we do anything about it? I will return to the second question in chapter 3. Here I will concentrate on the important and highly contentious debate as to whether, and if so how much, inequality and increasing inequality matter to human well-being.

1.5   Does Inequality Matter?

Why is there such an uncertain relationship between increasing average income and average contentment? Is it partly explained by increasing inequality in rich countries? The easy part of the answer is surely that when inequality takes the form of the bottom of the income distribution falling far away from the median, and when this fall away is so extreme that the bottom not only falls in relative terms but receives either no or very little increase in absolute income, it must matter a lot to the people at the bottom of the distribution. And that is not just a theoretical case; it is pretty much what has happened in the United States over the last 30 years, with the bottom 20 percent or so of the income distribution hardly participating in rising average prosperity. Even if we ignore any issues arising from relative-status anxiety, from competition for positional goods, or from congestion externalities, and simply allow for the fact that marginal units of income must be less important to the already rich than they would have been to the poorest, then, as Tony Atkinson has pointed out, the increase in the geometric mean of income is a better measure of increased welfare than the increase in the arithmetic mean.[24] (See figure 1.12.) And on that measure the US economy has delivered no improvement at all in the last 20 years.

Increasing US inequality at the lower end of the distribution, moreover, has had consequences that undoubtedly have contributed to a major setback to human welfare for many people around the world. As Raghuram Rajan points out in his recent book *Fault Lines*,[25] increasing inequality in the United States, which in the American political culture could not be offset by a distributional response, led instead to the deliberately encouraged palliative of risky credit extension to lower income groups. This explosion of sub-prime lending was a substantial contributor to the

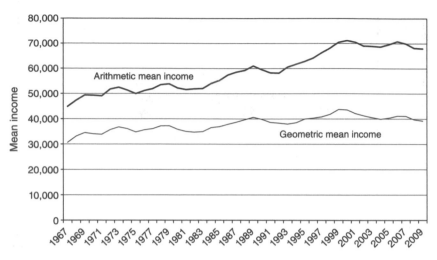

Figure 1.12
Two different perspectives on the growth of average US income. Source: Tony Atkinson, "Economics as a Moral Science," Joseph Rowntree Foundation Lecture, University of York, 2008.

financial crisis. Increasing inequality at the lower end of the income distribution as severe as that experienced in the United States in the last 30 years must matter a lot.

But increasing inequality could matter more generally, even if the poorest groups participate, at least to some degree, in rising absolute income. That is the proposition put forward by Kate Pickett and Richard Wilkinson in their recent book *The Spirit Level: Why More Equal Societies Almost Always Do Better*.[26] Across a whole range of indicators—including life expectancy, obesity, levels of community trust, violent crime, teenage pregnancy, and environmental sustainability—Pickett and Wilkinson find and illustrate with scatter diagrams (see, e.g.,, figures 1.13 and 1.14 here) adverse effects of income and wealth inequality. Those impacts, in turn, are explained both by the direct consequences for individual health, well-being, and social trust of intense relative-status competition and by the diminished ability of unequal societies to coalesce around the achievement of those elements of increased welfare that can be delivered only through collective action. Pickett and Wilkinson argue that the adverse consequences of inequality are so fundamental as to make unequal societies less attractive even for the winners at the top of the unequal pile.

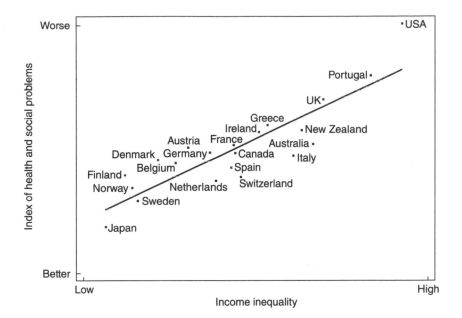

Figure 1.13
Health and social problems. Source: World Bank data, as referenced in Richard Wilkinson and Kate Pickett, *The Spirit Level* (Penguin, 2009).

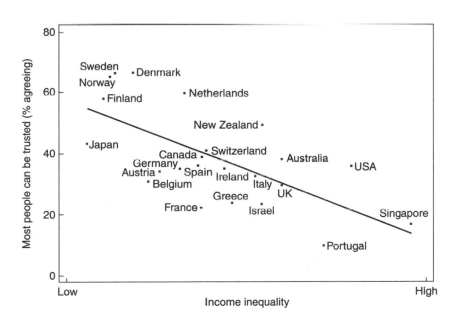

Figure 1.14
Most people can be trusted. Source: European and World Values Survey, as referenced in Wilkinson and Pickett, *The Spirit Level*.

The Spirit Level has been hailed by commentators across the political spectrum but has also been roundly criticized. David Cameron, in his Hugo Young lecture, endorsed its findings:

Research by Richard Wilkinson and Kate Pickett has shown that among the richest countries, it's the more unequal ones that do worse according to almost every quality of life indicator. In *The Spirit Level*, they show that per capita GDP is much less significant to a country's life expectancy, crime levels, literacy and health than the size of the gaps between the richest and poorest in the population. So the best indicator of a country's rank on these measures of general well-being is not the difference in wealth between them, but the difference in wealth within them.[27]

To the conservative (and Conservative) commentator Charles Moore, however, *The Spirit Level* is "more a socialist tract . . . than an objective analysis of poverty."[28] My own assessment is that the more thoughtful critics have made some valid points but have not by any means illustrated that inequality doesn't matter. Like John Kay (in the *Financial Times*), I think four reservations are appropriate[29]:

• It is clear from the scatter diagrams that the strength of the observed correlations varies greatly.

• Which way the causation flows is often debatable. For example, do high schools in the Southern states of the US have high dropout rates because there is great income inequality, or do those states have great income inequality because the dropout rates are high?

• We must always be cautious of believing that we have found *the* explanatory variable. Simply looking at many of the scatter diagrams makes one immediately aware of other possible factors. The Scandinavian countries, for instance, score far higher on many of the community and social relations factors than even Pickett and Wilkinson's equality-driven model would suggest. When we make comparisons with the United States, this raises the troubling issue of whether relative ethnic homogeneity is a powerful driver of trust.[30]

• I cannot see that Pickett and Wilkinson have managed to prove that unequal societies are bad for everyone's happiness, including that of the winners. Like John Kay, I feel that, although it would be satisfying to believe that excessive bank bonuses could, through their impact on society's cohesion, make even the recipients unhappy, I really doubt that such is the case. Particularly among the top few percent of the very well off, money enables people to isolate themselves and their families from many of the disadvantages an unequal society may bring.[31]

But with all these reservations noted, it remains a reasonable assessment that *The Spirit Level*, together with the huge body of evidence to which it makes reference (for instance, the work by Michael Marmot on the links between relative status and health), makes a powerful case that the degree of inequality in a society must have non-trivial consequences for many important aspects of human welfare.

And more generally, it is simply intuitively obvious that one's relative position in the income and status hierarchy matters a lot to one's sense of well-being. We know that people care about relative status: I certainly do to a significant extent, and I think almost everybody I have ever met does so to some degree. So if I ask myself whether I would rather live in Britain today on the average income of around £25,000 or in 1950 on an income of £20,000 per annum in today's real terms (a figure that would then have put me toward the top of the income distribution), I have no difficulty in imagining that I might prefer the latter even though it entails a lower absolute income. And it is easy to imagine that someone might prefer to live on £10,000 a year in a land where the average was £10,000 rather than on £11,000 a year in a land where the average was £20,000. Beyond some level of income that ensures the basic requirements of a good life (an adequate home, adequate clothing, good food, good health care, working hours that leave significant opportunities for leisure), one's relative income is an important driver of one's contentment, and concern about relative status is a significant driver of many people's anxiety. Inequality must matter, even if we conclude that that are no straightforward policies that will reduce it.

Of course, that leaves the issue of whether it *should* matter—whether relative-status anxiety should be treated as an understandable concern or dismissed as undesirable envy. After all, if the person imagined above prefers £10,000 per year when others have £10,000 rather than £11,000 when others have £20,000, then what is going on is that the additional £10,000 of everybody else's income is entering as a *negative* factor in the poorer person's utility function—a phenomenon that Martin Feldstein, in his 2005 presidential address to the American Economy Association, labeled "spiteful egalitarianism."[32]

That dismissal of the egalitarian case is debatable in philosophical terms. And it is particularly debatable if the less well off believe, sometimes with justification, that some of the highest incomes derive from activities that are more distributive than creative. People's attitudes toward inequality often seem to depend crucially on whether they intuitively understand and respect as worthwhile the "value" the highly skilled or the highly entrepreneurial have delivered. But even if we accept, with Feldstein, that envy is undesirable, and even if people feel relative-status anxiety in the face of *all* inequality, not differentiating between justified and unjustified, it would still be important for us to understand that this was the case. And this reality would carry consequences for whether economic growth, accompanied by increased inequality, is likely to deliver increased contentment. If people care a lot about relative status, that is a highly relevant fact for economists to understand, whether or not we think they should care.

Economists need to understand human behaviors and preferences as they are, not as they assume or wish them. And that indeed is the general conclusion I reach in this chapter. Economics must address the world as it is, not the world as we have assumed it to make our mathematics easy. It must ask questions about the end objectives of economic activity, even if answering these questions requires us to make judgments on the basis of imperfect empirical data, and even if the questions are only susceptible to incomplete and uncertain answers. Yes, the measurements of self-perceived happiness reported in Layard's book *Happiness*, or in Frey and Stutzer's book *Happiness and Economics*, are subject to significant methodological uncertainties, but at least they are asking the right questions, rather than simply assuming that we know the answer and that the answer is that growth is necessarily desirable.

In defining the objectives of economic activity, the instrumental conventional wisdom, which has dominated the policy application of economics for several decades, has simply assumed that maximizing growth in per capita GDP is an axiomatically desirable objective, and that inequality is justified because it helps maximize growth. But those assumptions are not clearly valid for already rich developed countries.

1.6   Revisiting Basic Frameworks

Deep inquiry into the objectives of economic activity and into the links between economic variables (such as income) and fundamental objectives (such as human well-being or welfare) is, therefore, essential to good economics, no matter how difficult. And once we pursue such inquiry, we may have to completely revise our assumptions about the framework of the marginal-utility curve:

• We begin with the standard assumption that, for any product or service, increasing value consumed delivers increasing utility, but subject to declining marginal returns. (See figure 1.9.)

• This tendency toward declining marginal utility may, however, be partially offset by the fact that entirely new products and services can create new demands to be satisfied, and new utility to be delivered by their consumption. (See figure 1.10.) But if we introduce behavioral assumptions relating to satiation, and to a hierarchy of human needs of changing nature and decreasing importance, we may still end up with an aggregate marginal-utility curve that is increasing but at a declining pace. (See figure 1.15.)

• But a number of mutually reinforcing factors then flatten, complicate, and kink the curve. First, it is highly likely, as Frey and Stutzer argue, that people adapt to levels of consumption already achieved, and that, once they have enjoyed a higher consumption level for a time, they need that higher consumption to deliver the same satisfaction as before. Aspiration levels increase, so that, although in the short term we are on a

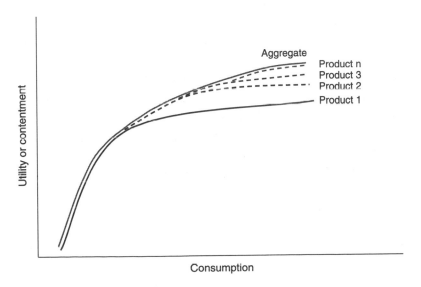

Figure 1.15
Aggregate diminishing marginal utility, driven by aggregate satiation.

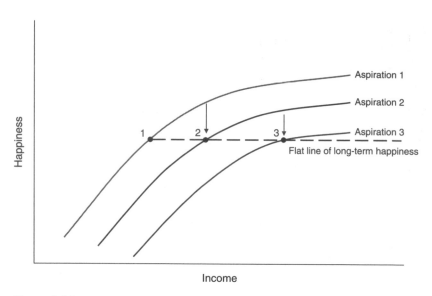

Figure 1.16
Happiness, income, and changing aspirations.

rising curve, in the long run we may be stuck on a horizontal line, as the curve itself adjusts. (See figure 1.16.) Second, it is clear that the idea that one person's utility is a function of that person's consumption alone is invalid. Our utility is also a function of others' income and consumption, both in some ways that even Feldstein would have to accept as relevant (competition for positional goods and congestion effects) and through the direct impact of relative-status competition, which Feldstein dismisses as "spiteful egalitarianism" but which may be a simple fact of life. Third, the tendency to adjust aspiration to achieved wealth and income may be so strong that at any one time any reduction in income or wealth is very strongly negative for welfare, even if increases are only slightly valued. (See figure 1.17.)

• Combining the first and the third factor, the long-term curve could therefore become closer to the shape shown in figure 1.18, with further increments in income delivering no necessarily permanent improvement in self-perceived well-being, but with any setback strongly negative, and with a factor that (for me at least) defies two-dimensional representation: my well-being dependent on my position relative to others as well as on my absolute income.

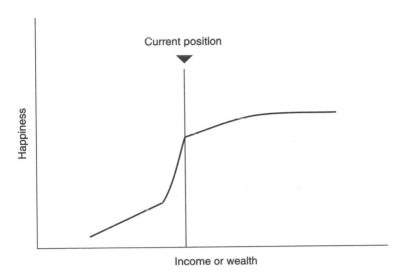

Figure 1.17
Happiness and already achieved income or wealth.

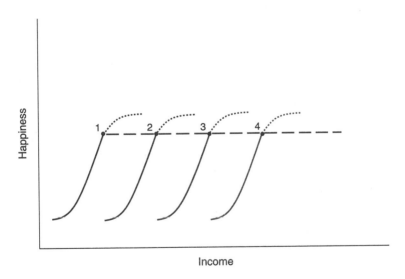

Figure 1.18
Happiness, already achieved income, and changing aspirations.

- But even this more complex shape may still seriously understate the complexity we face, since it still assumes that it is possible to plot a relationship between rising income and well-being without specifying the mix of consumption on which income is spent. Implicitly it therefore assumes that the marginal benefit of each different unit of additional consumption (whether spent on better health care, on more branded fashion goods, or on more road travel) is equal—an assumption apparently justified by the logic that if there were any difference between the marginal benefit of different categories of consumption, rational satisfaction-maximizing consumers would adjust their mix of consumption to bring marginal benefits into line. But this assumption may well not be valid: it is possible that the relationship between life satisfaction and income is different for different categories of consumption. If that were the case, we might expect to see different relationships between income and recorded life satisfaction in different countries that had (whether through private or public choice) made different decisions on how to spend the income benefits of economic growth. In those circumstances, economic growth would have the *potential* to deliver increases in life satisfaction, but there would be no certainty that it would do so.[33]

- We need to recognize that income alone is not the sole or indeed anything like the main determinant of self-perceived well-being. Even if we leave aside the many essentially non-economic factors that clearly are important—the vagaries of luck in family life, success in love and friendship, genetic predisposition—it is clear that access to employment should enter our framework as a crucial driver of happiness in itself, above and beyond the fact that employment helps deliver income.[34] Contrary to any free-market concept that unemployment imposes no utility loss because it results from a voluntary tradeoff between reduced income and increased leisure hours, all studies find that unemployment causes major unhappiness for the person affected, because work is for most people crucial to a sense of status and social relationships, and unemployment is a driver of low esteem and isolation. As I will argue in chapter 3, this has important consequences for many tradeoffs in public policy—for instance, in financial regulation, between policies that might maximize long-term growth and policies that maximize economic stability.

In sum, therefore, many of the assumptions and analytical frameworks that underpin the instrumental argument for free markets and inequality are either invalid or much weaker than is commonly supposed.

There is much uncertainty about what the objectives of economic activity should be and about how to pursue them: whether it is most useful to define the objective as happiness, and if it is, just how we measure and achieve happiness or well-being. And there are uncertainties about the implications of the empirical evidence of relationships between income and self-perceived well-being. But one thing we know with reasonable certainty is that increasing average per capita GDP beyond the levels achieved in rich developed countries doesn't, by itself, ensure significant increases in self-perceived well-being, and therefore is not a useful definition of the overriding objective of economic activity. As a result, the instrumental justification of free markets and inequality, which has played a major role in the political discourse of both right and left for the last 30 years, has largely lost its validity.

2

Financial Markets: Efficiency, Stability, and Income Distribution

In the first chapter, I considered the objectives of economic policy. In this chapter, I will turn to the issue of means, and in particular the role of markets.

Suppose that increasing per capita GDP is a sensible objective—and not just for middle-income and low-income countries, but also for high-income countries. How confident can we be that free markets are the way to deliver such growth? In particular, how important is financial-market liberalization, and what other consequences, good or ill, might free financial markets bring with them?

The proposition that markets drive economic efficiency is central to much of economics. Adam Smith illustrated that the "invisible hand" of the market drives efficient allocation of resources in a system of division of labor. Friedrich Hayek illustrated the central importance of the price system as an information processing mechanism more powerful than any centrally planned system could ever be. Kenneth Arrow and Gerard Debreu illustrated that complete and perfect markets deliver a Pareto-efficient equilibrium, in which no one person can be made better off without making someone else worse off. And the development of the efficient-market and rational-expectations hypotheses suggested that financial markets are in fact efficient, and that the conditions required for efficiency and for rational and stable equilibria apply even in contracts between the present and the future, which financial markets provide.

Together these ideas provided the intellectual underpinning for the powerful ideology of market liberalization and deregulation, an ideology that became increasingly dominant over the last several decades—the "Washington Consensus." According to it, almost all economic activities could be made more efficient if markets were allowed to operate with minimal "interference." Free trade, product-market liberalization, and structural reform of labor markets were all perceived as elements of a universally relevant policy approach, and free financial markets (the unrestricted flow of long-term and short-term capital) and financial deepening (access to a wide array of different financial markets and services) as essential to the efficient allocation of capital.

The political ideology was free-market capitalism. The intellectual underpinning was the concept of market completion—the idea that the more market contracts could exist, and the more freely, fairly, and transparently they could be struck, the closer we could get to the most efficient possible outcome, the one most favorable to human welfare.

One of the consequences of the capital-account and financial-market liberalization that followed was a very steep increase over the last 30 to 40 years in the relative scale of financial activities within the economy, with dramatic increases in capital flows, in the financial markets' trading volumes, and in the size of financial institutions' balance sheets relative to real non-financial activities.

During the run-up to the Asian crisis, capital flows to and from emerging countries grew rapidly, with an upsurge in equity portfolio flows, debt security flows, and cross-border bank claims. After the 1997 crisis, these capital flows resumed an even stronger upward path. (See figure 2.1.) That upsurge was matched by longer-term growth of financial capital flows between developed nations, accompanied over the last 30 years by a quite striking increase in the volume of foreign-exchange trading activity relative to global GDP and trade.

The crisis of 2008, meanwhile, came after several decades in which financial activity within developed economies—whether measured by the ratio of total bank assets to GDP, by the scale of credit and derivatives trading, or by the scale of trading in interest-rate derivatives—had increased dramatically. (See, for instance, figure 2.2.)

On a whole series of measures, therefore, the sheer scale of financial activity has increased dramatically, both in absolute terms and relative to real economic variables such as GDP, over the last 30 years. This followed several decades in which no such trend had been apparent.

That increasing scale of financial activity reflected in part the globalization of world trade and long-term capital flows and the world of floating exchange rates after the breakdown of the Bretton Woods system in the

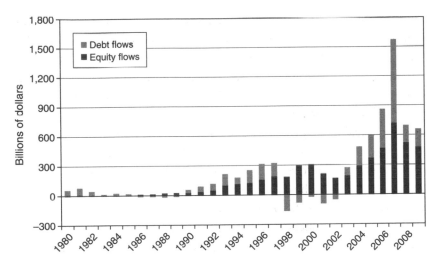

Figure 2.1
Gross private capital flows to emerging markets: debt versus equity. Equity includes direct investment and portfolio equity investment. Debt includes portfolio debt investment and other investment. Emerging markets include Argentina, Brazil, Chile, China, Colombia, the Czech Republic, Hungary, Hong Kong, India, Indonesia, Korea, Malaysia, Mexico, Peru, the Philippines, Poland, Russia, Singapore, South Africa, Thailand, Turkey, and Venezuela. Source: IMF International Financial Statistics.

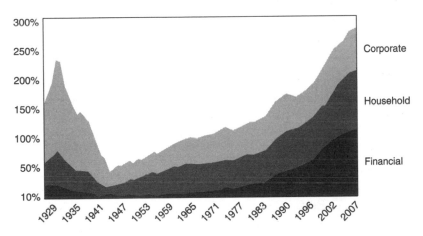

Figure 2.2
US debt as a percentage of GDP by borrower type. Source: Oliver Wyman.

early 1970s. But it was also deliberately fostered by policies of financial liberalization. The size and sophistication of financial sectors were seen as important positive drivers of national and global growth.

These drivers had the side effect of a dramatic increase in financial-sector remuneration relative to remuneration in the non-financial economy. Investment banking, financial trading, and hedge funds became the fields of choice for highly skilled people who wanted to get rich. Thomas Philippon and Ariell Reshef illustrate how the ratio of pay in the financial sector to pay for jobs of apparently equivalent skill has increased dramatically in the last 30 years, as indeed it did in the 1920s. (See figure 2.3.) And the growth of a larger and highly remunerated financial sector has been—in both the United States and the United Kingdom—a major cause of the overall increase in inequality discussed in chapter 1. But this didn't trouble the instrumental conventional wisdom, according to which it was obvious that this increased financial intensity and complexity, and the high pay that went with it, must be increasing the allocative efficiency of the

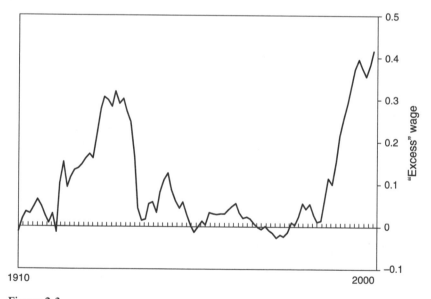

Figure 2.3
Historical "excess" wage in the US financial sector. Sources: T. Philippon and A. Reshef, Wages and Human Capital in the US Financial Industry: 1909–2006, NBER working paper 14644, 2009; A. Resh, as referenced by Andrew Haldane in *The Future of Finance* (LSE Report, 2010).

economy, driving an overall increase in prosperity at least as large as that accruing to the highly paid bankers.

The issues we must now address, after two terrible crashes in just 12 years, are whether this increasing scale of financial activity truly has been beneficial in its net effect, whether we can distinguish between beneficial elements and harmful elements of increased financial activities, and what tradeoffs are required in public policy to capture any benefits of increased financial liberalization while avoiding the destructive instability that seems at times to accompany it.

My focus in this chapter will therefore be on the financial-market aspects of liberalization and deregulation. But it is useful to place that within the wider context of the overall debate about the role of free markets in economic development. In the last 200 years, as I discussed in chapter 1, there has been an extraordinary and unique transformation in human living standards across the world. Some countries have achieved such high levels of income that further income growth may not be all that important; others are still midway through that transformation or at an early stage in it.

How important to this transformation have free markets been? Does the long-term historic record support the intellectual self-confidence of the Washington Consensus? It certainly supports a general preference for some category of market economy. Fully planned economies, with neither market-determined prices nor entrepreneurial freedom, have been remarkably unsuccessful—or at least have been subject to an atrophy effect, with initial spurts of growth turning later to stagnation, inefficiency, and corruption. And it is clear that access to foreign markets has typically played a major role in successful models of rapid economic catching up; to that extent, reasonably free trade is important. Furthermore, private entrepreneurship is clearly a powerful lever for driving the efficient delivery of the myriad of consumer goods and services that rich consumers desire. In nonmarket economies, restaurants and fashion goods were almost universally dire, and entrepreneurship has been far more effective than state planning in driving the innovations of information technology.

Thus, the overall case that markets have played a central role in this great transformation is a strong one. But it is also clear that there has been no one route to prosperity, and that some countries have achieved rapid economic growth while breaking many of the rules of the Washington

Consensus. Before the First World War, the United States achieved rapid industrial growth behind high tariff barriers. With elements of state-sponsored industrial strategy and significant tariffs, Japan from the 1950s to the 1970s and Korea from the 1960s to the 1990s achieved economic breakthroughs while breaking many of the rules of the subsequent Washington Consensus. China is stunningly successful with an eclectic economic model that combines elements of intense market competition and elements of state direction.

As Ha-Joon Chang points out in *23 Things They Don't Tell You About Capitalism*,[1] Thing 7 is that few successful rich countries got rich following the precepts of pure free-market economics.

So the general conclusion is that an assessment of the effectiveness of markets in driving economic efficiency and growth should be based on good economic history—on the open-minded analysis of a complex and varied set of historical experiences—rather than on a theoretical assumption that markets deliver efficiency because general equilibrium theory tells us that they should.

However, my focus here is not on all markets; it is on financial markets in particular. Have financial-market deregulation and the increase in financial intensity delivered an efficiency and growth dividend, and/or have they had other consequences, and are those consequences desirable? Is there in economic history a clear correlation between the financial intensity of an economy and the overall rate of economic growth?

At the macro level there is no clear and universal positive relationship. Carmen Reinhart and Kenneth Rogoff, in their recently published survey of eight centuries of financial folly, crashes, and debt defaults (*This Time It's Different*), identify the period from 1945 to the early 1970s as one of "financial repression" in which the role of the financial system was subdued in many countries.[2] And in some countries (for instance, one might argue, India) that "financial repression" probably was one of the market-restrictive policies that hampered economic growth. But in that period there were countries that achieved historically rapid growth with fairly "repressed" financial systems (for instance, Korea). And in the developed economies—the United States, Europe, Japan—that period of financial repression was one of significant and relatively stable growth, comparing fairly well with the subsequent 30 years of increased financial activity and financial liberalization.

Moreover, there doesn't appear to be any compelling quantitative proof that increased financial innovation over the last 30 years in the developed world has had a beneficial effect on output growth. A recent paper by Moritz Shularick and Alan Taylor documents the growth of leverage and credit extension that liberalization and innovation has helped facilitate but finds little empirical support for the proposition that this liberalization and innovation has led to a corresponding increase in trend growth rates for the countries in their sample.[3]

So the broad historical macro facts do not provide compelling evidence that an increase in the financial intensity of market economies is necessarily, always, and limitlessly beneficial for growth, even if we did believe that it was the desirable objective. To progress beyond this very general conclusion, however, we need to get more specific, both as to theory and as to the empirical record. In this chapter I aim to do that, addressing five issues: the theory of efficient and rational markets (and some compelling reasons to reject that theory), lessons from the Asian Crisis of 1997, lessons from the developed world's crash of 2008, financialization and income distribution (why bankers are paid so much), and some conclusions for policy and for the discipline of economics.

2.1 Efficient and Rational Markets: Neoclassical Theories versus Keynes/Minsky Theories

The predominant neoclassical school of economics has perceived increased financial activity—greater market liquidity, more active trading, financial innovation—as a broadly positive development. This is because extensive financial activity is essential to "complete" markets.[4] The first fundamental theorem of welfare economics, demonstrated mathematically by Kenneth Arrow and Gerard Debreu,[5] illustrates that a competitive equilibrium is efficient. But this is true only if markets are complete—that is, if there are markets that strike all possible desired contracts, including insurance contracts and investment contracts linking the present and the future, as well as markets for current goods, services, and labor. Therefore, the more liquid are financial markets and the more extensive is financial innovation, the more efficient the economy will be. Thus the following propositions follow:

- More liquid commodity futures markets are beneficial because they enable users and producers of commodities to hedge their risk more efficiently.
- Liquidity in the credit default swaps (CDS) market enables investors and issuers of corporate debt to achieve and continuously adapt their desired risk profile.
- The complex structured credit markets that arose in the mid 1990s were beneficial because they enabled investors to select the precise combination of risk, return, and liquidity that matched their specific preferences.
- The wider the set of options for linking suppliers of funds with users of funds (including via the provision of market liquidity which enables investors' time horizons to diverge from the contractual maturity of the instruments themselves), the more efficient will be the allocation of capital.

Initiatives to create market conditions consistent with these propositions could therefore be highly desirable, since such innovation "brings us closer to the Arrow-Debreu nirvana where all possible markets exist and are complete."[6]

Moreover, these advantages of financial markets are believed to apply not only within an economy but also between countries. The deeper and less restricted the markets for capital flows between countries, the more efficient the international allocation of capital will be, with globalization and financial liberalization therefore naturally and beneficially linked.

These propositions do not mean that there is *no* role for regulation of financial services and financial markets. Neoclassical theory specifies that competitive equilibrium conditions can be prevented by the existence of market imperfections and recognizes (in line with the Lancaster-Lipsey conditions) that if a specific market is imperfect then liberalization of other markets may be suboptimal.[7] But the neoclassical approach does tend to dictate a particular regulatory philosophy, in which policy makers ideally seek to identify the specific market imperfections preventing the attainment of complete and efficient markets, and in which regulatory intervention should ideally be focused not on banning products or dampening down the volatility of markets but on disclosure and transparency requirements that will ensure that markets are as efficient as they can be.

These propositions, and the strongly free-market implications drawn from them, have featured heavily in academic economics in the last several decades, though with dissenting voices always present. But they have been even more dominant among policy makers in some of the finance ministries, central banks, and regulatory bodies of the developed countries. The ideas that greater market liquidity was almost always beneficial, that financial innovation was to be encouraged because it was likely to expand investor and issuer choice, and that regulatory interventions had to be specifically justified by reference to the specific market imperfections they were designed to overcome were accepted elements of the "institutional DNA" of the United Kingdom's Financial Services Authority in the years before the crisis. And the predominant tendency of the International Monetary Fund, both at the time of the Asian crisis and in the run-up to the crisis of 2007–2009, was to emphasize the advantages of free capital flows and financial innovation, making reference to theories of market completion and allocative efficiency.

But this benign view of limitless financial deepening—of increased trading activity and innovation—is rejected by what we might label the Keynes/Minsky school of thought. Keynes, most famously in chapter 12 of *The General Theory*, argued that liquid financial markets did not ensure allocative efficiency through the attainment of a rational competitive equilibrium, but were instead subject, for inherent and unavoidable reasons, to self-reinforcing herd effects and momentum effects. Professional investment, he said, "may be likened to those newspaper competitions in which the competitors have to pick out the six prettiest faces from a hundred photographs, the prize being awarded to the competitor whose choice most nearly corresponds to the average preferences of the competitors as a whole. . . . It is not a case of choosing those which, to the best of one's judgement, are really the prettiest, nor even those which average opinion genuinely thinks the prettiest. We have reached the third degree where we devote our intelligences to anticipating what average opinion expects the average opinion to be. And there are some, I believe, who practise the fourth, fifth and higher degrees."[8]

Keynes therefore believed that the professional investor or trader, be it in equity markets, in currency markets, or (he would have said today) in the CDS market, is "forced to concern himself with the anticipation of impending changes, in the news and in the atmosphere, of the kind by which experience shows that the mass psychology of the market is most influenced." And he argued that pure speculation, not attached to fundamentals, could drive self-reinforcing bubbles, which not only served no useful allocative role but produced important destabilizing effects.

The potential scale of these self-reinforcing bubbles, and the economic harm they can do, has been documented extensively, first as early as 1852 by Charles MacKay in *Extraordinary Public Delusions and the Madness of Crowds*, later by Charles Kindleberger in *Manias, Panics, and Crashes*, and more recently by Robert Shiller in *Irrational Exuberance* (a book presciently issued at the height of the first Internet boom).[9-11] Together they and other writers have documented a historic record littered with equity, debt, property, and other markets that have moved far away from equilibrium levels—a record of huge booms followed by huge crashes, stretching from the Dutch tulip mania of 1635–1637 through the South Sea and Mississippi Scheme bubbles of the early 1700s, Wall Street's boom of the late 1920s and its crash of 1929, and the Asian emerging-markets crash of 1997 to the Internet boom and bust of 1998–2002.

Hyman Minsky argued persuasively that booms are inherent to the institutional structures and incentives of finance capitalism since a stretch of good economic times is likely to produce a shift in the relative balance of financial activity away from the those focused on hedging risks and on allocating capital efficiently and toward purely speculative activities that end in sudden collapses, debt deflation traps, and major economic disruption.[12]

Three somewhat distinct but also complementary sets of explanations have been put forward for these disequilibrium dynamics.

The first emphasizes the fact that human decision making cannot be seen as an entirely rational process, but is at times inherently instinctive and influenced by crowd psychology. The reasons for this are rooted in evolutionary biology and in the design of our brains. "When making difficult intertemporal decisions," Andrew Haldane writes, "we are quite literally in two minds."[13] We have a prefrontal cortex that is capable of patient rational analysis and a limbic system that disposes us to instinctive, emotional short-term responses. We are creatures of our evolved nature, which gives us a unique ability for rational thought but which also makes us naturally susceptible to herd effects—because keeping in with the herd, the crowd, the tribe, is an impulse that at some stage in our evolutionary history was important for survival. As George Akerlof and Robert Shiller explain in *Animal Spirits*, human psychology drives the economy, and we need to understand it as it is, not as the rational-expectations hypothesis assumes it.[14] There is no fully rational *Homo economicus.*

The second set of explanations, however, does not require that human beings act in an individually irrational fashion, but simply that information and contracting relationships are imperfect. For with information imperfections and imperfect structures of principal/agent relationships, it is quite possible for each individual to act in what seems to that individual, and indeed is, a perfectly rational self-interested fashion, but with the collectively resulting price movements subject to herd and momentum effects that take prices far from equilibrium levels. In Keynes's pretty-girl competition, after all, practicing the fourth, fifth, and higher degrees is entirely rational. This school of thought, therefore, need not reject the neoclassical assumption of a "rational economic man," but differs from the efficient-market and rational-expectations schools in recognizing that information imperfections are so inherent that no amount of market completion and increased transparency will ever overcome them.[15] Thus, for instance, the work of Roman Frydman and Michael Goldberg has illustrated that the essential assumption of the rational-expectations hypothesis—that there is a best model of how the economy works and that every rational agent will discover it and work in line with its assumptions—is logically impossible, and that as a result significant divergences of market prices from equilibrium values are bound to occur periodically.[16]

Third, one crucial reason why our knowledge of the future cannot be perfect is that the future is characterized by inherent irreducible uncertainty, not by mathematically modelable risk. That distinction, made in Frank Knight's "Risk, Uncertainty and Profit" and in Keynes's "Treatise on Probability," is fundamental, but is too often ignored not only by mainstream economics but also by Keynes's "practical men."[17,18] Major investment banks, for instance, use "value at risk" methodologies to assess potential losses from trading positions. These methodologies assume that the observed frequency distribution of market price movements over recent periods carries strong inferences for the probability distribution of future possible movements, and thus can be used to estimate the maximum losses that could be incurred at any given level of confidence (e.g., the maximum loss that would occur 99 percent or 99.9 percent of the time). But this assumption has turned out to be dangerous for three reasons. First, it was often assumed, for ease of modeling, that the distributions were "normal." Second, the reliance on observations of the recent past introduced a systematic tendency to pro-cyclical risk assessment. Third, and most crucially, the very idea that in social science we can derive the objective probability distribution of future outcomes from observation of past outcomes is a philosophical category error, since no probability distribution of future outcomes objectively exists. As Mervyn King and others put it in a recent paper, since beliefs and behavior adjust over time in response to changes in the economic and social environment, "there are probably few genuinely 'deep' (and therefore stable) parameters or relationships in economics, as distinct from in the physical sciences, where the laws of gravity are as good an approximation to reality one day as the next."[19]

It is therefore notable that the school of thought that we might broadly label as Keynes/Minsky is not characterized by a single unifying theory equivalent to that of neoclassical equilibrium. As a result, it is not easy to derive from this way (or rather these ways) of seeing the world a simple and universally applicable set of criteria for deciding appropriate regulatory intervention, such as can be derived from the neoclassical approach. But it is better to live in the real world of complexities imperfectly understood than to construct for ourselves an intellectually elegant set of assumptions that don't accord with real-world phenomena. And the evidence from the crises of 1997 and of 2007–2009, to which I will now turn, suggests that we should be highly skeptical about the benefits of general and limitless financial liberalization.

2.2   The Asian Crisis of 1997

In relation to the 1997 crisis, the crucial contested issue in economics is that of the benefits and disadvantages of short-term financial capital flows. As I have already noted, these flows increased dramatically in the decade before the 1997 crisis, and the dominant conventional wisdom of the time (as expressed, for instance, in the attitude of the International Monetary Fund), was that these flows were positive. This was based on the neoclassical argument that capital flows in general (including short-term portfolio flows as well as long-term direct investment) help achieve a more efficient global allocation of capital, linking savers to business investments in a more efficient fashion.[20]

Indeed, it was in September of 1997, right in the middle of the Asian crisis, that the IMF, at a meeting held in Hong Kong, proposed that capital-account liberalization should be made a binding commitment of IMF membership, going beyond the commitment to current-account convertibility included within the IMF's founding articles.

But although this was the conventional wisdom, many studies have cast doubt on whether free movement of capital, and in particular of short-term capital, has a positive effect on growth. The challenge has been launched on both empirical and theoretical grounds.

• The empirical evidence has been assessed by a working group of the Committee on the Global Financial System.[21] That group notes that "despite the numerous cross-country attempts to analyze the effects of capital account liberalization, there appears to be only limited evidence that supports the notion that liberalization enhances growth." Some of the protagonists in this debate, including Dani Rodrik and Jagdish Bhagwati, would go further and say that there is no compelling evidence at all.[22, 23] Even those who broadly support capital-account liberalization have therefore tended to argue that liberalization *could be* beneficial under specific circumstances, rather than that it has been demonstrably beneficial in all cases.

• Dani Rodrik and Arvind Subramanian have highlighted one reason why the apparent case for financial globalization might not apply in today's circumstances. In the first period of financial globalization—the 40 years or so before the First World War—international capital flows, to a significant extent, took the form of outflows from rich developed countries (in particular the United Kingdom) and inflows to commodity-producing countries that lacked adequate domestic savings to develop their industries. But, as Rodrik and Subramanian point out, this is not the recent pattern. Net capital flows, indeed, have been as likely to be *from* poorer developing countries *to* rich developed ones as vice versa, and developing countries' savings rates have usually not been a binding constraint on growth. The case in favor of capital flows, therefore, has to assert that intensive two-way flows of capital facilitate a more efficient allocation, rather than asserting that a net flow of finance to developing countries is important to the development process.

• Meanwhile, many analyses have illustrated that short-term financial capital flows, particularly into debt securities and via cross-border bank lending, can be extremely volatile, subject to what Reinhart and Rogoff label "bonanzas" followed by "sudden stops." Bonanzas seem to be strongly influenced by self-reinforcing herd effects, with some investors caught up in over-optimistic stories about a country's prospects while others quite rationally seek to ride the self-reinforcing appreciation of the local currency or asset markets for as long as the bonanza lasts. Sudden stops and outflows, meanwhile, are even more strongly self-reinforcing, with a contagious collapse of confidence affecting not only countries in relation to which there is a least some new information that might reasonably carry inference but also countries treated by investors as in the same broad category. As a result, markets for domestic financial assets in emerging countries and foreign-exchange markets can be characterized by multiple and fragile equilibria, as was illustrated by the movement of foreign-exchange rates for the Thai bhat, the Korean won, and the Indonesian rupee in 1997.

• In addition, volatile short-term capital flows can complicate the conduct of domestic monetary policy, forcing authorities to choose whether to allow undesirably rapid growth of domestic credit and money or to accept exchange-rate appreciation that may undermine the competitiveness of traded sectors in a fashion not justified by long-term fundamentals. Moreover, short-term capital inflows, particularly of bank debt, can drive disruptive asset-price booms in local markets, such as that for commercial real estate.

• As a result, a compelling argument has been developed that the balance of benefits and disadvantages of capital flows varies by type of flow—an argument well summarized by the Committee on the Global Financial System. This suggests a hierarchy in which long-term capital flows are better than short-term flows, direct investment is better than portfolio investment, and equity is better than debt, with short-term inter-bank flows the least beneficial and potentially the most disruptive.

Together, these arguments make a compelling case for believing that the positive benefits of short-term capital flows may be very slight, even in the absence of shocks, and that these benefits can be significantly outweighed by the adverse effects of financial shocks.

Against this criticism, not only has the counter-defense of capital-flow liberalization sought to deny the reality of potentially volatile capital flows; it has also argued that this potential arises only because of fundamental deficiencies in, for instance, the credibility of government's fiscal and monetary policy, or the quality of domestic financial system regulation and governance. These arguments recognize—in line with the Lancaster and Lipsey second-best theory—that market liberalization can be harmful if applied in a context where many other market imperfections and distortions exist. But this insight is then used to support the argument that capital-flow liberalization *can* be a good thing provided that appropriate supplementary reforms are made in the appropriate sequence. This "conditions and sequencing" argument enables believers in the free-market creed to hold that the faults in the system revealed by the crisis of 1997 ultimately lay not in too much market liberalization, and not in the inherent instability of markets, but in inadequately complete application of free-market precepts.

This argument between those who believe that the potentially harmful volatility of financial markets is inherent and unfixable and those who believe that it can be fixed if credible policies are in place and well communicated is an old one. In 1943, in a paper written in advance of the Bretton Woods deliberations, the economist Ragnar Nurkse reviewed the floating-exchange rate regimes of the early 1920s and concluded in particular that movements in the exchange rate of the French franc between 1924 and 1926 illustrated "the dangers of cumulative and self-aggravating movements [which] instead of promoting adjustments in the balance of payments, are apt to intensify any natural disequilibrium and to produce what may be termed 'explosive' conditions of instability." But Nurkse's account was met by the counter-argument of Milton Friedman et al. that this apparently self-fulfilling unstable speculation was a rational response to the uncertainties of French policy, and that the correct conclusion is that policy should be appropriate, well communicated, and credible.[24]

In view of these alternative arguments, it is, as Barry Eichengreen has noted, not possible to *prove* which argument is correct, unless we are able to look directly into the minds of financial speculators—and in view of Andrew Haldane's insight that the individual speculator might be "of two minds" it might not even be possible then. But although proof is ultimately unattainable, there are three compelling arguments for not seeing the "conditions and sequencing" argument as at all conclusive. The first of these is Rodrik and Subramanian's point that, even if in theory such "conditions and sequencing" could remove the disadvantages of short-term capital flows, we have to make decisions in a real world, where governments are equipped with imperfect tools and are subject to short-term political pressures, and where their ability ever to get "conditions and sequencing" right is inherently imperfect. Second, Charles Kindleberger and other economic historians have documented the tendency of many different types of markets to be subject to manias, panics, and crashes. Third, John Maynard Keynes, Hyman Minsky, George Soros, Joseph Stiglitz, Robert Shiller, and others have advanced explanations of how a combination of rational incentives and psychological tendencies can be expected to produce self-reinforcing momentum effects.[25]

Overall, therefore, the case that short-term capital-flow liberalization is beneficial is (as Bhagwati argued in his famous 1998 article "The Capital Myth: The Difference between Trade in Widgets and Dollars") based more on ideology and argument by axiom than on any empirical evidence— though it is also undoubtedly, as Bhagwati argued, based on interests. For what we saw with capital-flow liberalization in the 1990s (as with domestic financial liberalization in developed countries) was the assertion of a self-confident ideology that also happened to be in the direct commercial interest of large financial-services firms with powerful political influence in the major and developed economies, particularly the United States.

That combination of ideology and interests has proposed a conventional wisdom of self-equilibrating exchange rates and optimal capital flows. Instead we need to recognize that in global short-term capital and related foreign-exchange markets we face the risk of potential instability and overshooting. What we should do about that is less obvious. It doesn't necessarily follow that comprehensive controls on the flow of capital are a required or a feasible response. There is a reasonable argument that, although the theoretical and empirical case against constraints on short-term capital flows is poor, the pragmatic case against them (or at least against their comprehensive application) is quite strong, simply because they may be unenforceable and may tend to produce other distortions.[26] But we should at least recognize the world as it is, not as efficient-market models assume it. In that real world, foreign-exchange markets and short-term capital flows are not necessarily self-equilibrating, and at times they are subject to inherent and self-reinforcing instability.

2.3   The Developed World's Financial Crash of 2007–2009

The 1997 crash created an acute awareness of the potential instability of financial markets and caused a policy reaction in some emerging-market countries that contributed to the 2008 crash. Developing countries sought to insure themselves against future crises via policies that produced large current-account surpluses and the accumulation of foreign-exchange reserves. And the investment of these reserves in low-risk instruments, such as US Treasury bonds and agency debt, drove global risk-free rates down, facilitating credit extension in several developed countries (particularly the United States) and provoking a search for yield uplift, which was met (so it seemed) by the cleverness of complex financial innovation.

But these macroeconomic-imbalance-driven developments interacted with, and gave further impetus to, trends that were already underway in developed economies' financial systems and whose common feature was a startling increase in the scale and complexity of financial activities. I referred earlier to the huge increases in the value of foreign-exchange trading activity relative to global GDP from the early 1970s on; some of this trading related to the currencies of emerging-market countries, but most of it to the currencies of the major developed economies. I also mentioned the very steep increase in inter-financial-institution balance-sheet claims that began in the 1970s and continued up to the crisis. From the 1980s on, these trends were accompanied by the following:

• The emergence of a huge market in interest-rate derivatives, with the notional value of over-the-counter interest-rate contracts rising from close to zero in 1987 to more than $400 trillion in 2007.

• Enormous growth from the mid 1990s in a series of interrelated credit markets. New "technologies" of pooling and tranching enabled the growth of a more than $2 trillion market in private label asset-backed securities, supporting a new "originate and distribute" model of credit extension. Global CDSs outstanding grew from zero in the mid 1990s to more than $60 trillion in 2007, with the scale of this "hedging" activity massively outpacing the growth of the underlying credit instruments which CDS contracts enabled investors or issuers to hedge. And collateralized debt obligations (CDOs) grew from zero in the early 1990s to more than $250 billion by 2005, with the notable development of synthetic CDOs—credit exposures manufactured through the use of the CDS market, rather than out of the underlying liabilities of non-financial counterparties.

• Immense growth of commodities futures trading, with, for example, the volume of oil futures traded growing from far less than the volume of physical oil produced and consumed in the world in the early 1980s to more than ten times the volume in 2008.

Just as with the growth of international capital flows and of related foreign-exchange trading, so too with many other financial activities: the last two to three decades have seen a dramatic increase in the scale of financial activity relative to the real economy, accompanied by complex financial innovation.

And just as with international capital flows, so too with increased financial intensity and innovation: the predominant official view before the crisis was that this increased financial intensity had delivered important economic benefits.

A chapter in the IMF's Global Financial Stability Review of April 2006 devoted to assessing "the influence of credit derivatives and structured credit markets on financial stability" described the policy makers' conventional wisdom, which rested quite explicitly on the principal assumptions of neoclassical theory:

• It noted with approval that credit derivatives "enhance the transparency of the market's collective view of credit risks [and thus] provide valuable information about broad credit conditions and increasingly set the marginal price of credit." In the neoclassical model, such price transparency delivers greater market efficiency and takes us closer to the efficiency-maximizing equilibrium.

• It noted with approval that such greater transparency "improves market discipline," mirroring some arguments for short-term capital flows, which see market discipline on domestic policy makers as a strongly positive function.

• It argued that these benefits, far from being accompanied by any dangers of instability, were likely to be accompanied by greater financial stability, since more complete markets make possible a better dispersion of credit and liquidity risks to those investors whose preferences and own liabilities make them the most suitable holders. "There is a growing recognition," it therefore noted, "that the dispersion of credit risk by banks to a broader and more diverse group of investors has helped make the banking and overall financial system more resilient. The improved resilience may be seen in fewer bank failures and more consistent credit provision."

The IMF was not alone in having confidence in the benefits of financial liberalization. There were, of course, some economists who raised fundamental objections to the conventional wisdom—William White, Raghuram Rajan, Nouriel Roubini, and Robert Shiller, for instance.[27] And concerns were often expressed, including within the IMF Global Financial Stability Report from which I have quoted, about specific developments in particular credit markets and about the capacity of risk-management systems always to cope with increased complexity. But the predominant view in policy-making circles was not only sanguine about increased financial intensity and financial innovation but positive. And the dominant intellectual ideology of the day was largely embraced by regulators who, as a result, were highly susceptible to the argument that if a particular regulation threatened financial innovation or market liquidity then it was, by definition, inappropriate.

It is now obvious that this dominant ideology was wrong, failing to allow for the potential downside of the instability that increased financial complexity might produce. And it failed to consider this possibility because it was based on the assumption that financial markets are rational and equilibrating, rejecting or ignoring the Keynes/Minsky insight that financial markets can be subject to self-reinforcing swings of irrational exuberance and then despair.

Thus, the IMF, along with many other authorities, welcomed the increased transparency of credit prices provided by the CDS market, and saw it as a benefit that the marginal price of credit (i.e., the pricing of loans to the real economy) could more accurately reflect "the market's collective view of credit risk." But the market's collective view of credit risk proved to be subject to an extreme irrationality that played havoc with the real economy. Figure 2.4 shows CDS spreads for a composite of major financial groups between 2002 and 2008. It illustrates that the market's collective view was that risks to bank creditworthiness had fallen steadily between 2002 and 2007, reaching a historical low in the early summer of 2007, the very eve of the worst financial crisis in 70 years. Neither CDS spreads nor bank equity prices provided any forewarning of impending disaster.

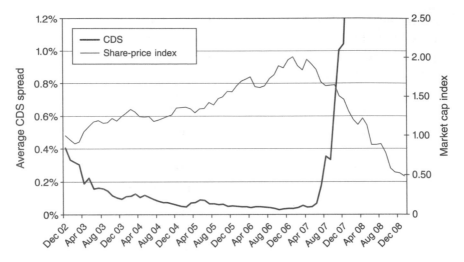

Figure 2.4
Financial firms' CDS and share prices. Firms included Ambac, Aviva, Banco Santander, Barclays, Berkshire Hathaway, Bradford & Bingley, Citigroup, Deutsche Bank, Fortis, HBOS, Lehman Brothers, Merrill Lynch, Morgan Stanley, National Australia Bank, Royal Bank of Scotland, and UBS. CDS series peaks at 6.54 percent in September of 2008. Source: Moody's KMV, FSA Calculations.

Instead they validated and strongly reinforced a surge of over-exuberant and under-priced credit extension to the real economy.

CDS prices did indeed help bring the marginal price of credit in line with the collective judgment of the market. The problem was that the market's collective judgment was wrong. In the market for credit securities and credit derivatives, just as with international capital flows, intense financial activity can generate bonanzas of over-exuberant financing which are followed by sudden stops and contagious loss of confidence.

But alongside this now obvious point, it is also worth noting that even the supposed benefits of increased financial intensity—the benefits we might wish to trade off against the dangers of instability—are at best unproven. As with capital-flow liberalization, so with structured credit and credit derivatives: the argument that such derivatives delivered allocative efficiency, benefits, or direct welfare benefits because investors were better able to meet their preferences for precise combinations of risk, return and liquidity has tended to be made by axiom, with no attempt to consider how great the value of such benefits could be.

Of course it would be extremely difficult to measure that benefit in any empirical fashion, other than by means of very macro analysis such as that of Schularick and Taylor. But we should at least recognize that any benefits must be subject to declining marginal returns, and that if liquidity up to a point is beneficial, there must be a point beyond which still further increases in liquidity can deliver only the most minimal incremental benefits. In an article published in the *Financial Times* in August of 2010, Benjamin Friedman of Harvard University questioned how much economic value added could arise from arbitrageurs' being able to spot microscopic divergences in market prices a few seconds (or now, with algorithmic trading, milliseconds) before other arbitrageurs do the same, and thus reaching a Keynesian "pretty girl" judgment a millisecond before everybody else reaches the same judgment.[28] Friedman's challenge has been too often absent in responses to arguments that condemn possible regulatory approaches on the grounds that they will reduce liquidity in specific markets.

It is therefore clear that in financial markets market completion and increased liquidity may, under some circumstances, bring with them the disadvantage of increased instability, and it seems likely that any benefits of market liquidity and completion must be subject to diminishing marginal returns. What this might imply for optimal policy will be discussed later. But let us turn now to one other striking effect of increased financial intensity: the extent to which it has been accompanied by high factor incomes and returns for both labor and capital and, as a result, has been a significant contributor to the increased inequality considered in chapter 1.

2.4   Financial Intensity and Income Distribution

The value added of financial activity forms part of GDP, entering either as an end product or service consumed directly by individuals or as an intermediate product or service used as input to the production activities of other businesses. Working out what that contribution is, and what meaning to attach to the figures estimated within national income accounts, is extremely complex. Indeed, the meaning of calculated GDP is in general far less clear than is often supposed. But the complexities and uncertainties are at their most acute in respect of financial services—a fact reflected in the title of Andrew Haldane's contribution to the recent London School of Economics report *The Future of Finance*: "What Is the Contribution of the Financial Sector: Miracle or Mirage?"

But if we take the figures at face value, the increase in the relative role of the financial sector over the last 160 years of market capitalism is noteworthy. In the United Kingdom, over those 160 years, the measured gross value added of the financial sector appears to have outperformed the growth of the whole economy by more than 2 percent per annum. (See figure 2.5.) Some of the outperformance isn't surprising—for reasons I'll return to, some financial deepening is likely to be a value-creative feature of the early and middle stages of economic development. But what is striking is the pattern within the 160 years (table 2.1): very large outperformance from 1856 to 1913, underperformance from 1914 to 1970, and then outperformance over the last 38 years. And although the growth rate of the overall economy was also lower across the whole period 1914–1970, that period included two hugely destructive world wars. The years from 1945 to 1970 were ones of rapid growth, but of much lower financial intensity than in the subsequent years.

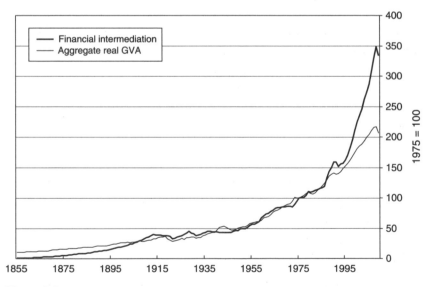

Figure 2.5
UK financial intermediation and aggregate real gross value added (GVA). Source: Andrew Haldane, *The Future of Finance* (LSE Report, 2010).

Table 2.1
Average annual growth rate of financial intermediation (real values). Sources: Office for National Statistics and Bank of England calculations, as referenced by Andrew Haldane in *The Future of Finance* (LSE Report, 2010).

	GVA: Aggregate	GVA: Financial Intermediation	Difference (pp)
1856–1913	2.0	7.6	5.6
1914–1970	1.9	1.5	−0.4
1971–2008	2.4	3.8	1.4

Trends in the United States show a somewhat similar but more dramatic pattern (figure 2.6): a 160-year increase in financial intensity from 1 percent to 8 percent of GDP, but with two very strong upswings—in the 1920s and over the last 30 years—and, as with the United Kingdom, a period (1945–1970) of rapid overall economic growth but nowhere near as much financial intensity as in the last 30 years.

These increases in financial intensity have been accompanied by high factor income for those involved. There was a dramatic increase in the level of financial sector pay relative to that in the non-financial economy (figure 2.3), and financial corporations also appeared to deliver high though volatile returns to shareholders. Haldane's chapter in *The Future of Finance* draws attention to a dramatic increase in return on equity in UK finance as we moved from the financial repression of the 1940s, the 1950s, and the 1960s to the financial deregulation of the 1970s and later. (See figure 2.7.)

Why did this increase in return both to highly skilled labor and to capital occur? The dominant ideology of market completion and liberalization assumes by axiom that it must have derived from an increase in the importance of value-creative financial activities within the economy—the need in a more complex world for finance to perform more complex functions, and the development by finance of "technologies" which contributed to improved allocative efficiency and economic growth. But there are at least four other potential explanations:

• Retail financial services (but also some wholesale services to institutional investors and businesses) are subject both to opacity of margins and to deep asymmetries of knowledge and market power between producers and consumers—a classic formula for above-normal returns.

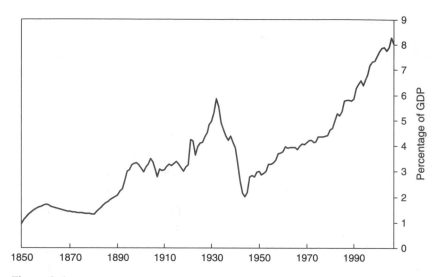

Figure 2.6
Share of the financial industry in US GDP. Source: T. Philippon, *The Evolution of the US Financial Industry from 1860 to 2007: Theory and Evidence*, 2008, as referenced by Andrew Haldane in *The Future of Finance* (LSE Report, 2010).

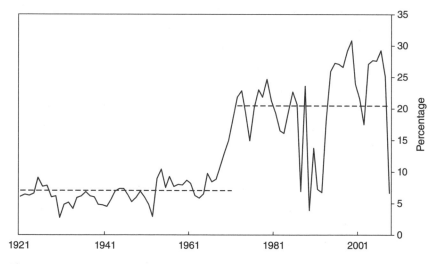

Figure 2.7
Return on equity in finance. Sources: F. Capie and M. Billings, BBA and Bank of England calculations, 2004, as referenced by Andrew Haldane in *The Future of Finance* (LSE Report, 2010).

• Complex and opaque options are common features of many financial products and contracts. Structured products may appear to provide "alpha" (i.e., higher return without higher risk), but do so only because several years of superior return come with the hidden danger of occasional dramatic losses for which the producer carries no liability. And if banks are treated as "too big to fail," so that bank debt holders can be confident that public bailouts of failing banks will protect them from loss, that represents a put option onto the taxpayer, allowing banks and shadow banks to operate with high leverage that increases their returns in good years.

• Regulatory and tax arbitrage activities are widespread. In the parlance of investment banking, 'creative' is used far too often to describe activities—undoubtedly requiring considerable mathematical, logical, and legal skill—that are, in Roger Bootle's terms, purely distributive. This redistribution is achieved via either regulatory arbitrage or tax arbitrage. (Regulatory arbitrage is the design of products and legal structures to alter the regulatory treatment even when the economic substance is unchanged, thus undermining regulatory attempts to limit the "too big to fail" put option. Tax arbitrage is the design of products and legal structures to reduce tax payments without any change in economic activity, redistributing income from the generality of taxpayers to the employees and shareholders of financial companies.)

• The financial system collectively, via its own intra-financial system trading activities, tends to create volatility against which the non-financial economy then has to hedge, paying the financial system for the service: an initially zero-sum activity (proprietary trading against one another) which then becomes positive-sum for the financial industry and negative-sum for all others.[29]

What then is the balance between the real value added and the distributive rent extraction? We don't know. But we do know that there is more potential for finance to generate redistributive rents than exists in most other sectors of the economy.

And a lot of those rents stick to the highly skilled employees. The shareholders get high returns, but at the expense (on Haldane's figures) of higher risk. It is the explosion of investment bank and trading remuneration that is the more striking phenomenon, and the phenomenon now attracting very significant social concern.

Within the conventional wisdom of beneficial market completion, no basis for concern can exist. Highly skilled labor will deliver high marginal product, and will be highly paid as a result, but theory tells us that in efficient markets it cannot be paid more than its marginal social product. Thus, although you may think that those proprietary traders are making money at your expense, at the end of some long and complex chain of market completion and increased allocative efficiency GDP will have increased by at least the amount that they have been paid: they are richer and no one else is worse off. If bankers are paid more than research scientists, that must be because their marginal social product is higher.

But this logic is invalid for two reasons. First, the presence of "distributive" activities can result in marginal private product being far higher than marginal social product—indeed, if complexity brings with it instability, marginal private product can be high even when marginal social product is negative. Second, pay is influenced by the measurability of marginal product as well as by the size of marginal product. In many areas of economic activity, marginal individual product is extremely difficult to calculate: How much is that research team really contributing to the company's long-term health, and how much each individual scientist within it? Is that Human Resources manager really producing value-creative improvements in employee morale and motivation? But in financial trading, the return seems clear and quantified at the end of the year. And it is because that quantification is apparently clear that the dynamics of labor-market negotiation mean that a lot of the benefit sticks to the employee.

The higher the share of complex financial services in our economy, the greater therefore the danger that highly skilled people will be attracted to activities whose social impact is simply distributive but for which the private returns are very large.

This, of course, is not the same as saying that *all* financial activity is "socially useless." Financial systems perform important and valuable roles in any market economy, and their development played a crucial role in the great transformation of the last two centuries. But it does mean that a financial system could grow beyond its socially optimal size. And when combined with the indirect nature of finance's value to the economy, it creates the danger that finance can become unconstrained by the ethical constraints that can limit the proliferation of purely redistributive or harmful activities in other areas of the economy.

Finance (both wholesale and retail) involves many activities that are, in Roger Bootle's terms, creative." (See chapter 1.) But to an even greater extent than in other sectors, the "creative value" is delivered indirectly and in association with distributive activities. Thus, for instance, providing liquidity through market-making in commodities or foreign exchange can play an economically valuable role in facilitating creative economic activities (e.g., value-creative physical trade), but this "creative" effect is achieved indirectly and in association with activities (position-taking to make a profit) that are also distributive. Although this mix of directly distributive and indirectly creative activities is found in many sectors of the economy, it is a particularly dominant feature of financial activities. And the fact that the value creation is indirect means that participants are usually detached from any direct experience of the useful end-results, and typically measure their success in entirely monetary terms.

As Raghuram Rajan points out in chapter 6 of *Fault Lines*, this detachment from any direct contact with the end-value created means that profit and pay received tend to become the *sole* measures of success, unbalanced by the other factors that enter the motivation of people in other areas of the economy (e.g., the restaurateur who wants to get rich but is also proud of his food and service, or the saleswoman who wants to get the order but is also proud of the product she is selling). The sole focus on monetary measures of success, in turn, tends to create a culture in which ethical constraints on potentially harmful or aggressively redistributive activities are weakened.

As Rajan puts it, "the personal checks and balances that most of us bring to bear when we are employed in other activities—we ask ourselves if we are producing a socially useful product—operate less well in finance because, with few exceptions, making money is the raison d'être of the financier." This absence of naturally arising checks and balances creates a potentially legitimate role for regulatory intervention: not only to ensure that financial systems are stable, but also to lean against clear rent-extraction activities. It also raises important issues for the top management of financial institutions. For instance, it is unclear how top management of wholesale banks can credibly seek to convince society that their activities are "socially useful" if significant profits are earned from activities whose primary functions are to minimize tax or to arbitrage regulatory constraints and which are thus entirely distributive.

Conclusions

The impact of financial-market liberalization, and indeed the importance of market liberalization more generally, is much more complex than the dominant conventional wisdom of the last several decades has asserted. For correct understanding, for policy, or for the discipline of economics, what overall conclusions can we draw? I suggest four.

• Imperfect markets are different. Tolstoy's novel *Anna Karenina* opens with the famous line "All happy families are happy in the same way: all unhappy families unhappy in their own specific way." Similarly, in Paul Krugman's neat adaptation, "all perfect markets are perfect in the same way: all imperfect markets imperfect in their own different way." But truly perfect markets exist only in economists' models; in the real world, markets are imperfect. But within imperfect markets there is a range from those that work well enough for a laissez-faire approach to be broadly valid to those for which market failure or imperfection is extreme and inherent. The market for restaurants works pretty well. The best way to ensure a range of restaurants that provide us with variety, incentives for good service, and enjoyment of changing ambience and menu is to let entrepreneurship do its business—let thousands of flowers bloom, some to succeed and some to wilt. Anyone who doubts that didn't visit a restaurant in the Soviet bloc before the Berlin Wall came down. But other markets are inherently more imperfect, and inherently volatile. And financial markets—which link the present to the future under conditions of inherent irreducible uncertainty—are hugely susceptible to imperfection, irrationality, and the proliferation of distributive rather than social-value-creative activities.

• The benefits of financial-market liberalization and deepening vary by stage of development. I said earlier that part of the growth in the value of financial services within GDP, illustrated in figures 2.5 and 2.6 and in table 2.1, almost certainly was conducive to economic growth. The development of the British banking system probably was, as Walter Bagehot argued in *Lombard Street*, among the factors that gave the British economy an advantage against some Continental economies—one of the drivers of the great transformation in its early stages.[30] A number of studies have illustrated either cross-sectional or time-series correlations between the development of basic banking and financial systems and economic growth.[31] The development of a banking system able to connect savings to investment opportunities in rural India is important to Indian growth. And in China, both growth in credit as a percentage of GDP and the development of markets in health insurance and life insurance will better enable households to smooth their consumption across the life cycle and to pool insurance risks, and could play an important role in freeing Chinese people from the burden of excessively high savings rates. That would allow them to enjoy the fruits of economic growth, and would help to unwind a huge source of global macroeconomic imbalance and potential instability.[32] But it is quite reasonable to believe that liberalization delivers significant benefits up to a point but not beyond that point; that there is a point of optimality; that, for instance, good basic credit provision matters a lot and credit derivatives are less important; that a functioning market providing adequate hour-by-hour liquidity is valuable, but that there is no social value in being able to buy and sell within a millisecond. At the early stages of growth, growth matters a lot to human well-being; at the earlier stages of financial liberalization, financial liberalization stimulates growth and widens the range of choice available.[33] Later in the development process, the last increment of extra growth matters much less to human welfare, and further financial liberalization is less likely to deliver increments in growth and more likely to produce the proliferation of rent-extraction opportunities.

• In rich economies, stability matters a lot; small further increases in allocative efficiency matter less. Thus, policy should be heavily focused on ensuring macroeconomic and financial stability and very wary of financial innovation if it carries with it any risk of increased instability. Within rich economies, public policy should focus on creating stable environments in which human freedom to choose can be exercised, and downsides and setbacks are minimized, rather than on driving a maximization of GDP as the overriding objective in itself.

• What implications follow for the discipline of economics? That is a topic to which I will return at the end of chapter 3, looking at the implications for both the definition of economic objectives and the analysis of economic means. But from the above analysis of the nature of financial markets, and of the failure of the conventional wisdom in the crash of 2008, four implications follow:

Economists should study human behavior as it is, not as they find it easy to model. Robert Lucas, a leading exponent of the rational-expectations hypothesis, has referred to a theory as something that can be put on a computer and run, enabling "the construction of a mechanical artificial world populated by interacting robots which economics typically studies."[34] But reliance on the study of that world and those robots won't enlighten economists about the real world. The real world is populated by humans whose brains include a prefrontal cortex capable of ratiocination and a limbic system in which we are coded by evolution to act in deeply instinctive and emotional ways. Economists should study that reality.

Economists should study financial markets as they actually operate, not as they assume them to operate—observing the way in which information is actually processed, observing the serial correlations, bonanzas, and sudden stops, not assuming these away as noise around the edges of efficient and rational markets. And that means that descriptive economics, such as Akerlof and Shiller's *Animal Spirits*, is as important as mathematical economics.

Economic history matters. Students of economics should read Charles MacKay and Charles Kindleberger, and should study the history of the Wall Street Crash as well as the theory and the mathematics required to formalize it.

Good economics should not attempt to arrive at any all-encompassing model or theory, because the real world isn't like that. Should we understand the instability of financial markets in terms of human behavior and brains which are part emotional and part rational, or in terms of information asymmetry so deep that financial markets would be unstable even if populated by Robert Lucas's robots, or in terms of Knightian inherent irreducible uncertainty? The answer is all three.

In short, real-world economics cannot be monolithic. That puts it at a disadvantage in the competition of ideas. Many people are drawn to all-encompassing intellectual systems, elegant in their basic theoretical structure, that appear to provide clear and consistent answers to all policy questions; that's why, in Bhagwati's terms, ideology matters as well as interest, and why, in Keynes's words, "practical men, who believe themselves quite exempt from any intellectual influences, are usually the slaves of some defunct economist." But we need to fight against the allure of complete systems, accepting and communicating the fact that—although good economics can help us understand the world, mitigate specific risks, and think through appropriate responses to continually changing social problems—good economics is never going to provide the certain, simple, and complete answers that the pre-crisis conventional wisdom claimed it could.

3

Economic Freedom, Public Policy, and the Discipline of Economics

I began chapter 1 by describing the dominant political and economic conventional wisdoms of the last 30 years, which together provided an instrumental justification of free markets: the idea that free markets and strong market incentives to economic efficiency are good because they will make societies richer on average, the idea that getting richer is by definition good for human welfare, and the idea that, in turn, inequality is a by-product of a dynamic free market, justified because and to the extent that free markets with substantial inequality generate faster growth.

But in fact, as was set out in chapter 1, we cannot be confident that economic growth beyond some level of per capita GDP will necessarily deliver significant and sustained increases in welfare, and it seems highly likely that inequality can be a major cause of human anxiety and unhappiness that no amount of growth will dispel. And, as was set out in chapter 2, some forms of market liberalization—particularly in financial markets—may not deliver increased economic efficiency, and may result in both increased instability and increased inequality, the net benefit of liberalization being highly dependent on precise details and precise circumstances. The pre-crisis justification of financial liberalization as beneficial because it maximized global economic efficiency and thus growth is therefore dangerously simplistic.

The instrumental case advanced for free-market capitalism and market liberalization—a case that has been dominant for 30 years—is therefore unconvincing both in its specification of objectives and in its prescription of means. For some people, the logical alternative might seem to be a sort of radical green egalitarianism in which economic growth would be seen as not only unimportant but positively harmful, radical action to reduce inequality would be justified by the sort of analysis that Wilkinson and

Pickett present, and markets would be regarded as being of little value and as tending to generate high levels of inequality.

But this chapter is going to disappoint radical green egalitarians. For I believe there is a strong argument for a market economy, which will tend to result in growth and which will tend to generate non-trivial levels of inequality. But the argument is quite different from that advanced in the last 30 years, resting primarily not on the instrumental benefits of economic freedom for prosperity but on a human desire for change and economic freedom as ends in themselves—ends, however, that will have to be balanced against other potentially desirable objectives.

In this chapter I will argue that measured economic growth should not be the overriding objective, but that it is the likely and acceptable, though not in itself very important, by-product of two desirable things: economic freedom and the avoidance of involuntary unemployment. I will then explore possible policy implications of my conclusions—both those that are clear and those for which the issue is clear but the resolution is not. Third, I will consider the implications for the discipline of economics, a subject that Lionel Robbins himself addressed 79 years ago in his *Essay on the Nature and Significance of Economic Science*.

3.1   Growth as a Decreasingly Important By-Product of Freedom

In chapter 1, I argued that it is not clear that economic growth beyond that already achieved in rich developed countries will deliver further significant and sustained improvements in average or aggregate happiness, or welfare, or utility, or however we define the objective. But there remain at least three reasons why economic growth may, in some circumstances, be positively desirable, and three further reasons in favor, not of growth per se, but of economic freedom and markets, with growth a by-product of other desirable objectives.

Three arguments for growth

Growth in low-income countries
The first argument for growth is the most obvious, though it is not directly relevant to the issues I am seeking to address in this book. Economic growth, even if measured via the imperfect devices of national income

accounting, is very important to welfare in countries still well short of satiation. The same analysis that casts doubts on the importance of income beyond a certain level suggests that it is likely to be very important up to that level. Classic economic growth still matters a lot in China and in other emerging middle-income countries, and it matters a very great deal in Africa. And the instrumental argument in favor of free markets and inequality is still valid to the extent that reasonably free markets, incentives for entrepreneurship, and some significant resulting inequality are elements of a formula that tends to deliver growth in developing countries (an empirical issue that one should approach with an open mind). But in this chapter I am not focusing on those problems of middle-income and lower-income development.

"Good growth" can deliver well-being

The second argument is that although the empirical evidence and *a priori* logic discussed in chapter 1 cast doubt on the assumption that economic growth necessarily and limitlessly delivers increased human contentment, they don't prove that economic growth has no potential to deliver increased well-being even in rich countries. The cross-country comparison data, in particular, are compatible with the assumption that increased growth has some mild benefit, though with a weak correlation and with other important factors clearly at work. And since some factors that researchers have identified as strongly associated with self-perceived well-being can be enhanced by growth (for example, health can be improved through innovation and the allocation of resources to health services made possible by growth), there is also an *a priori* argument for believing that some permanent increases in human well-being *could* be delivered via economic growth. The crucial issue is therefore whether the actual path of growth followed delivers the products and services most likely to result in sustained increases in well-being.

The poor in rich countries

Even in rich countries, there are many people who are relatively poor, some of them still below the level beyond which it is likely that higher absolute income becomes less important to increasing welfare. So don't we need growth in order to raise the income position of the poor? Doesn't a rising tide lift all boats? Am I, and other doubters about the limitless and certain value of growth, open to the charge "It's all right for you, one of the better-off, but wouldn't you want to maximize economic growth if you were at the bottom of the income distribution?" But the precise answer to that question depends crucially on the relative importance to the welfare of the poor of absolute income versus relative income and relative social position. If what matters is absolute income alone, then an instrumental argument for free-market growth could be justified even if it resulted in high inequality, as long as the absolute income of the poorest progressed. But if (as was suggested in chapter 1) both relative income and absolute income matter, and increasingly so as the general level of income rises, then the argument that says "Don't worry about increasing inequality if it helps create wealth," even if empirically correct, is not compelling.

In these circumstances, economic growth is relevant to the position of the poorest only and to the extent that it could, at least in theory, help ameliorate relative deprivation. It may do so because it makes redistribution more acceptable. Richer and middle-income people in rich societies are unlikely to be made significantly and permanently happier by further increases in average national per capita GDP, but the same logic that leads to that conclusion also suggests that people can be made unhappy by setbacks to levels of income and wealth already attained. Any attempt to redistribute income to the less well-off in order to address relative deprivation within a static economy will therefore be strongly resisted. In a growing economy, such redistribution may be more feasible.

That creates an instrumental justification for growth, but one that is valid only if it is combined with action to address the relative position of the least well-off. If instead the argument is made that we need lower taxes on entrepreneurs, market liberalization, and lower public expenditures in order to spur growth, that we should be unconcerned by increasing inequality because it is a necessary concomitant to growth, and that growth is essential because it still matters to the relatively poor, we should recognize the internal inconsistency of that argument.

Three arguments for markets and economic freedom

Markets, economic growth, and economic regression
Economic freedom can be justified, not because it is essential to achieve further growth, but because economies may tend to regress without it.

Where economic freedom to innovate, to improve productivity, to set up new businesses, and to compete is absent, we sometimes see not just slow or no growth but absolute regression, falling living standards, declining public infrastructure, and declining levels of health. That was true of the Soviet Union in its final years of stagnation. A planned economy without economic freedom fails not only because economic planning cannot replicate the effectiveness of the price mechanism as a means of processing information (Hayek's famous insight) but also because, without markets and market incentives, human behavior changes in two ways. First, there is a pervasive tendency across society for people to cease to care about the quality of the product or service they are delivering if there is no market incentive or sanction at the firm or the individual level to make them care. Second, there is a strong tendency for elite groups to channel their natural human tendency for relative-status competition into positively harmful activities—aggrandizement of organizational units or personal power for its own sake, and outright corruption. As Keynes puts it in *The General Theory*, one of the benefits of the market and of significant inequality is that "dangerous human proclivities can be canalized into comparatively harmless channels by the existence of opportunities for money making and private wealth, which if they cannot be satisfied in this way, may find their outlet in cruelty, the reckless pursuit of personal power and authority and other forms of self-aggrandizement. It is better that man should tyrannize over his bank balance than over his fellow citizens."[1] This may seem a very negative justification for markets and resulting inequality, but even this negative justification is, I think, more compelling than the instrumental argument that markets are good and inequality is acceptable because they produce growth, which in turn delivers happiness.

The journey matters, not the destination

Once we start thinking of growth not as an objective but as the result of the expression of natural human proclivities, that also leads us to a direct and positive justification of economic freedom as an end in itself—a point that Keynes himself also made in in *The General Theory*: "[T]here are valuable human activities which require the motive of money-making and the environment of private ownership for their full fruition." And those valuable human activities need not be directly linked to any theory that growth is required to deliver happiness. Rather, competition, innovation, and the desire to do things better, more efficiently, or just differently should be recognized as ends in themselves.

As I suggested in chapter 1, there is no sound basis for believing that devoting additional resources to ever-increasing competition in fashion-intensive and design-intensive goods, or to branding, will make people permanently happier. But the possibility of change, the fact that fashions change every year, the fact that there are new ideas, and the fact that there is competition for people's attention may well be essential to contentment in a rich, liberal, open society.

More fundamentally, expectations of technological progress, innovation, improved productivity, and new production possibilities can be important to our sense of well-being, even if no permanent increase in happiness results after the expectation is satisfied. My marginal-utility curve may continually adjust downward, so that no permanent increase in happiness ever occurs, but at *any one time* it is upward sloping. Since I know that the electronic gadgetry I own today has not made me permanently happier than I was with a much smaller array 20 years ago, I suspect that the latest generation of computer tablets and high-definition TVs will not make me permanently happier in the future. But I would be made unhappy if the economy suddenly became static and if products and services didn't in some way get better or merely change. And this is not just because of the temporary buzz one might expect to get from new products; it is because product innovation is in itself an expression of the spirit of inquiry that is a defining characteristic of the modern world, inherent to the great transformation and to the world it created.

The journey matters, not just the destination.

Economic freedom as an end in itself
Economic freedom on both the consumption side and the production side—not only the right to choose what to consume but also the right to set up a new company, to work for oneself, and to compete with new ideas—should be recognized as a desirable objective in and of itself, not because of any prosperity dividend it delivers.

The Soviet Union was ultimately a failure in terms of human welfare not just, and perhaps not even primarily, because it failed to deliver increased GDP growth, but because it stymied the natural human desire to be allowed to make one's own choices. Amartya Sen makes the point in the first chapter of *Development as Freedom*.[2] Let us suppose, he asks, that, contrary to Hayek's proposition, a centralized Soviet economy of directed labor and no entrepreneurial freedom had been as effective as a market economy at delivering GDP growth. Would that have been an equally desirable outcome? The answer is surely No, because, as Sen puts it, "the freedom of people to act as they like in deciding on where to work, what to produce, what to consume" is in and of itself an important aspect of freedom. As Sen writes, "the merit of the market does not lie only in its capacity to generate more efficient culmination outcomes, but in the processes by which those outcomes are achieved."

The crucial justifications for economic freedom and for markets, therefore, are independent of the allocative efficiency benefits of markets, and they are still valid even if in rich developed countries we have reached a point where further growth in aggregate GDP has a reduced potential to increase aggregate human welfare or happiness.

But if economic freedom, a spirit of inquiry, and a desire for change are combined with the attainment of one other undoubtedly desirable objective, the absence of involuntary unemployment, measured GDP growth is likely to result as a by-product.

Growing income may not make people happier; however, involuntary unemployment tends to make them unhappy, both because it involves a setback to already attained levels of income and wealth and because it involves loss of social contact within the workplace and loss of status. But the exercise of economic freedom will tend to generate improvements in productive efficiency as more efficient firms replace less efficient ones, and that will lead to involuntary unemployment unless there is aggregate growth.

Growth in rich societies, as measured by standard national income accounting, should not, therefore, be an overt objective of economic policy. Rather, it should be seen as an acceptable consequence, sometimes mildly beneficial but sometimes harmful, of two underlying desirable objectives: economic freedom and a wide set of employment opportunities. And inequality, rather than being instrumentally justifiable because and to the extent that it delivers growth, is justifiable because and to the extent that it is the unavoidable concomitant of economic freedom.

Thus, as I stated earlier in this chapter, my position will disappoint some radical green egalitarians, as it is neutral toward growth, rather than opposed to it, and it accepts some significant inequality as unavoidable. There is, I believe, a compelling liberal argument for economic freedom, for markets. And from economic freedom will follow both economic growth and significant inequality.

But if this is the real justification for the market economy, an essentially moral and political justification rather than a narrowly economic one, then we cannot avoid debating political choices that the instrumental conventional wisdom sought to sweep away—for instance, political choices relating to the degree of inequality. And across a wide range of policy issues, the conclusions I reached in chapters 1 and 2 on the objectives and means of economic activity carry policy implications significantly different from those that appeared to follow from the instrumental justification of markets as a means to maximize growth. So let me first suggest four areas of policy in which there are clear implications—and let me then suggest two areas in which the optimal way forward is more difficult to determine but in which we should at least recognize open issues, rather than close off debates with simplistic assumptions.

3.2   Implications for Policy

Given what we know or at least strongly suspect about the drivers of human contentment, and about the shape of marginal-utility curves discussed at the end of chapter 1, public policy should place strong emphasis on maximizing stability and minimizing downsides, on maximizing public choice, and on minimizing the intensity of zero-sum competition. Those principles carry important implications for four specific areas of policy.

Maximizing stability and minimizing downsides: macroeconomic management and financial regulation

When summarizing my argument in chapter 1, I said that long-term growth maximization should not be the principle objective of public policy, but that from today's starting point, in the middle of a recession, short-to-medium-term growth is undoubtedly very important. That may seem a contradiction, but it is not.

We have reasons to doubt that further increments in average income will make people in already rich societies significantly and permanently happier, but we have good reasons to believe that setbacks to already attained income and wealth make people unhappy. Pay cuts are more negative to happiness than pay increases are permanently positive. Losing a home as a result of mortgage default and repossession makes people very unhappy. Involuntary unemployment has a major negative effect, both because of its impact on income and because of the direct negative effect of lost self-esteem and social interaction.

So economic stability—avoiding severe recessions—matters a lot. And if we do fall into recession, with output and employment falling below full capacity levels, growth back toward high capacity utilization matters a lot—because it is essential if we are to avoid prolonged harmful employment, but also because recessions create high government debt, and once we have that, we face an "imperative to grow" that doesn't otherwise exist.

The idea that we "need to grow" in order to afford high levels of future public expenditure is largely fallacious; growth doesn't enable us to afford more teachers and nurses, because their incomes tend to grow with average earnings.[3] But indebtedness does create a growth imperative. Without growth, debt servicing and debt reduction require expenditure reductions and tax increases, which impose resented and resisted setbacks to people's existing income and wealth.

How we can achieve growth out of the present recession, in the face of debt burdens that must be reduced, is an extremely difficult question, and one on which I will not comment here. But the objective is clear: Growth out of a recession matters, even though maximizing long-term growth is not a sensible objective. These are not contradictory statements; they derive from the same analysis of the drivers of human satisfaction.

But it is far better, of course, not to fall into severe recession in the first place, and better to have a stable economy, even if at the margin that requires a small sacrifice of long-term growth. This has clear and important implications for decisions on future financial regulation.

In chapter 2, I described how, in the decades before the crisis, we were told that increased financial intensity and financial innovation would, by complex indirect processes, increase the allocative efficiency of the economy and thus spur economic growth. Sometimes we were also told (bizarrely, in retrospect) that the same developments would increase stability. But at times the proposition was more buccaneering—there would be no reward without risk, but the dynamic world of financial liberalization would deliver efficiency improvements sufficient to compensate us for any downside of instability.

In chapter 2, I questioned whether any such economic efficiency benefit was actually achieved, or whether much financial activity was not distributive in form, at best zero-sum, and sometimes rent-extracting. But let us suppose for now that financial liberalization, intensification, and innovation could somehow increase the medium-term achievable growth rate at the cost of increased instability. Then the argument set out in chapter 1 suggests that it might still have been wise to forgo those benefits. If financial intensity and sophistication increase the attainable medium-term growth rate marginally (say, from say 2 percent to 2.05 percent), the benefit to long-term human happiness may be minimal,[4] but if they increase the volatility of the economy, thereby increasing the possibility of recessionary setbacks, those setbacks may have potentially serious consequences for the well-being of many people.

In our reform of financial regulation, we should therefore have a very strong bias toward increased system stability—arguably, indeed, a greater focus on stability than is assumed in the macroeconomic assessments made so far. In those assessments, conducted by the Financial Services Authority (which regulates the UK's financial services industry) and by the Bank for International Settlements, we have attempted to compare the benefit of reduced probability of recessions with the possible cost to economic growth of higher capital requirements.[5, 6] A crucial choice in that comparison is the discount rate—the relative price by which we compare benefits in one time period and costs in another. And, in line with standard assumptions, we have used one constant discount rate to compare those costs and benefits, allowing for timing differences, but not allowing for the possible severe asymmetry of people's happiness response to incremental income gains versus setbacks to income already attained. If we allowed for that asymmetry, we would place far greater weight on the avoidance of setbacks than our current constant discount rates assume, and our estimates of optimal bank capital requirements would be higher than those we have so far calculated.

Once maximizing growth is no longer the objective, minimizing setbacks becomes an important objective. Macroeconomic management to ensure a stable economy matters a lot; overall economic policies to maximize the long-term growth rate are far less important.

And that, in turn, carries implications for the questions "How should we view GDP figures?" and "To what policy decisions are GDP figures useful inputs?"

• GDP figures are almost useless as measures of long-term changes in human well-being. Even as measures of long-term changes in what we think they measure ("real income") they are highly imperfect, because they depend on conventions and assumptions that are to a degree arbitrary. How do we measure the value of financial services? Can we distinguish effectively between distributive or rent-extracting activities and "creative" activities? If we spend more of our income on housing, competing for a positional good and driving up the price, should that show up as an increase in inflation, or as a form of real income, even though we are not in aggregate consuming any more housing services than before? As we get richer, as measured by national income accounting measures, it becomes decreasingly clear what long-term trends in GDP are telling us, or whether we can infer much at all from comparisons of rich countries' per capita GDPs.

• But as measures of short-run changes in the level of activity, and thus as information relevant to optimal macro management (hitting inflation targets and ensuring recovery from recessions), they are relevant and valid, because in the short run the impact of arbitrary accounting conventions makes little difference. Quarter-by-quarter changes in GDP tell us something useful; changes in per capita GDP over decades tell us much less. Lionel Robbins, writing at a time when the techniques of national income accounting were in their infancy, made this point: "Both the concept of world money and national money income have strict significance only for monetary theory."[7]

Minimizing downsides: policies to mitigate climate change
The objective of minimizing downsides is also highly relevant to optimal climate-change policy.

Climate change could impose severe costs on humanity—severe reductions in human well-being. But reducing greenhouse-gas emissions to limit the harmful impacts will involve some sacrifice of future growth. How to compare the costs and benefits? That was the question handed to Nicholas Stern, and his response was the brilliant report *The Economics of Climate Change*.[8]

On the costs to growth, Stern argued that we could achieve radical cuts in emissions, of the scale needed to contain global warming to 2°C, at a cost to global and UK GDP in 2050 of only about 1 to 2 percentage points, a sacrifice which would mean the UK growing at perhaps 1.95 percent per annum from 2005 to 2050 rather than the 2.0 percent per annum that might otherwise be achieved—a difference whose impact on human well-being, in the developed world at least, could well be nil, given uncertainties of the link between growth in measured GDP and growth in well-being or happiness.

Against these costs, the benefits of avoiding climate change—i.e., avoiding the costs which it would impose—are more difficult to quantify. Some (changes in agricultural yields and in the cost of food) are conceptually easy to envisage but are difficult to quantify because of the uncertainty of regional climate-change models. But some are more inherently uncertain because they are contingent on social and political reactions—the danger that changes in agricultural yields may be so significant as to produce movements of people, and the political instability that could result. And one of the most important factors to consider is the small probability of catastrophic events, again an area where quantification is inherently judgmental.

But Stern argued persuasively that a reasonable estimate placed the net present value of harm avoided far above the cost of mitigation—the equivalent of 5–20 percent of global GDP in harm avoided versus something like 1 percent of costs.

That judgment, however, necessarily depended on the use of a discount rate to compare costs and benefits over time. And Stern's choice of a discount rate proved controversial, because the discount rate makes a lot of difference.[9] Valued with a discount rate of 2 percent real, £1,000 of benefits in 2150 are worth £59 today: discounted at 4 percent, they are worth £3.67. And on that basis 100 percent of GDP in 2150 is worth only 6 percent of GDP today, so that if you believed that money income fully measures human utility, and that climate change would destroy the world entirely in 2150, you still wouldn't pay more than 6 percent of today's GDP to stop that from happening.

So the discount rate matters. But the logic of declining marginal utility can be used to argue for a *high* discount rate: If further growth delivers little additional benefit, why sacrifice present prosperity for the benefit of future richer people? Let them, out of the additional income they will hardly value, pay the costs of climate change. The higher the elasticity of the marginal utility of consumption (i.e., the flatter the curve becomes), the higher it seems the discount rate should be.

But that logic is flawed, because it assumes that those who will suffer from climate change will be richer than those who make the sacrifice and because it assumes that the detriments of climate change can be offset by future higher income. And neither of those assumptions is valid. Even if climate change is moderate, the future sufferers may be poorer than we are today, because they may be concentrated in the poorest countries; if that is true, the discount rate should actually be negative. If climate change is catastrophic, it will reduce everyone's well-being below present levels—and that small probability of catastrophic loss should also enter the calculation at a negative discount rate. And if the losses from climate change include losses of perceived well-being deriving directly from environmental degradation—the loss I might feel if coral reefs or major animal species were to be lost—then the idea that we can count our future additional material prosperity as offsetting such losses is invalid.[10]

In thinking about climate change, we need to place high value on minimizing the risks of downsides for the poorest, of catastrophic downsides for all, and of downsides that cannot be offset by increased consumption, given that, in the rich developed world, increased consumption per se gives an uncertain human happiness dividend.

If we re-calculate Nicholas Stern's cautious figures to allow for those downsides, the developed world should commit to radical reduction of carbon emissions even if the cost to measured growth is much higher than the 1–2 percent that Stern estimated.

Maximizing public choice

Climate change is a global environmental problem, a global externality. Economic growth and change arising from economic freedom can also, of course, impose very local environmental impacts relevant to human well-being—for example, the impact of new roads on beautiful countryside via visual or noise pollution, or the impact of out-of-town shopping centers on the survival of a village's stores or the vibrancy of a town's center. But for consumers who have cars (the majority in most rich countries) those shopping centers may also reduce travel times, or may offer lower prices or greater choice.[11]

A crucial issue is, therefore, how such tradeoffs of costs and benefits should be decided. If you believe that growth in per capita GDP is the prime objective, the tradeoff should place great weight on the importance of national productivity growth. And that apparent imperative was indeed given considerable weight in recent years, with studies of the productivity gap between the United Kingdom and the United States revealing that much of it lay in retailing and wholesale distribution. That seemed to imply that planning should be deregulated in the UK.

But if the last increments of growth in average income are of no necessary value to human happiness, and if what matters is the exercise of economic freedom and the possibility of change and technological advance, *not* the maximization of measured income as an end in itself, then the imperative of national productivity enhancement should have little if any weight. Instead, decisions on planning philosophy should be based on political debate, either national or local, over the balance of benefits and costs that different policies would produce—benefits and costs that may not be reducible to a single quantitative figure. Such political debate, in turn, has value not only because the factors to be brought into account are inherently judgmental but also, as Frey and Stutzer point out, because participation in political processes, including local political processes, is in itself something that people value, something that seems to deliver life satisfaction. People gain utility from participation in decision making in itself as well as from outcomes more attuned to local needs.[12]

As Sen says, freedom to choose is a merit of the market in and of itself, independent of its "culmination outcomes"; but that choice is also important with respect to public goods—preserved countryside, attractive and vibrant urban space—that can only be delivered collectively.

The instrumental conventional wisdom emphasizes the imperative of national productivity enhancement. An important finding of more subtle economic thinking is that no such *imperative* exists but that there are choices which people should be free to make.

Minimizing competition for positional goods: welcome population stabilization

I argued in chapter 1 that one of the reasons why we should not expect economic growth to deliver continually increasing human well-being is that as we get richer individual well-being is influenced by the income of others—by congestion externalities and by the need to devote an increasing proportion of income to competition for locally specific positional goods.

As we get richer, we choose to travel more, but everybody else's travel degrades our quality of experience. We hope to travel to uncrowded beaches, countryside, or ski slopes, but the richer everybody else gets, the more crowded those places are. We devote more of our income to competing to buy houses in the most pleasant areas, but increased average income doesn't help us achieve this, only increased relative income. Meanwhile, urban and road developments driven by increased prosperity can degrade some aspects of housing amenity, thereby increasing the importance of winning the relative-income competition.

This is inherent to increasing income levels, but the pressures get worse and the intensity of relative competition increases with increasing population density. If, as now forecast by the United Nations Medium Projection, the British population increases from 62 million to 72 million by 2050, these pressures will increase and relative-status competition will become more severe. Conversely, if the British population stabilizes through some combination of a lower birth rate and lower immigration, aspects of that competition will become less intense.

And if the global population stabilizes at around 10 billion, as the UN Medium Variant Projection (2008) suggests, the negative environmental and congestion externalities of growth will be less than if the population continues to increase. This is so obvious that it is odd that it needs saying. But it does need saying, because the conventional wisdom of a growth-maximization imperative is frequently used to argue the inverse—that Britain and other European countries "need more immigrants" or "need to raise their birth rates," since otherwise the per capita GDP growth rate or (even more absurd) the aggregate national growth rate will decline.[13, 14] But to accept that logic is to trap us in a hamster wheel of ever increasing population density, ever more intense externalities, and ever more intense competition for relative income and positional goods.

What follows is not that there should be a policy to manage birth rates down, but simply that we should accept as fortunate the remarkably universal finding that fertility rates tend to fall to around or a bit below replacement levels if women are educated and free to make their own decisions. Nor does a preference for population stability resolve optimal immigration policy: the freedom to migrate, particularly for those threatened by political persecution, is a freedom that no liberal can restrict lightly. But it does mean that the instrumentalist argument for immigration—that immigration is good because it will help drive the growth rate—is a very poor one.

The Common Principle

Across a wide range of policy areas—financial regulation, climate change, local planning decisions, demographic concerns—optimal policy choices change significantly when we shift from growth as the objective to growth as the result of other ends desirable in themselves: economic freedom and a spirit of inquiry, change, and innovation.

The aim should not be to maximize growth, but to create a stable economic environment in which freedom to choose can be expressed, both individually and via political processes, while minimizing the downsides and managing the externalities that the exercise of freedom can sometimes produce.

But although having that as the aim carries some specific policy implications, such as the four discussed above, it doesn't provide answers to all questions. Rather, on some issues, it tells us what is not true or what is not resolvable by economics alone, leaving us with difficult social and political choices. That is true of two issues in particular: whether some forms of growth and some types of consumption are better for human well-being than others, and what we should do about inequality.

Good and bad growth?

We have no good reason to believe that growth in average income beyond the level already achieved in rich developed countries will *necessarily* deliver improvements in human well-being or in self-perceived happiness. Over the long term, the aggregate marginal-utility curve may be quite flat.

But that still leaves the possibility (indeed the probability) that different aspects of consumption, different goods to which we could devote increased income, are characterized by very differently shaped curves (figure 3.1)—that there are some consumption categories to which we could devote our income for which there is as yet no declining marginal return, others for which the curve has flattened, and others for which, beyond some level, rising income results in a decline in aggregate utility.

Figure 3.1
Marginal utilities of various "goods."

In the first category we might find good health and expectation of a long and healthy life. As Richard Layard has highlighted, poor mental health is a very important driver of unhappiness.[15] Early death of loved ones is also and obviously a major cause of unhappiness. Not surprisingly, when people are asked to evaluate the importance of various factors to their self-contentment, good health often achieves the highest rating. And economic growth can—through better diet, better health-care resources, better sports facilities, a better-designed environment, and better mental-health practices—help deliver good physical and mental health.

In the second category we might find expenditures on branded fashion goods. Such expenditures, driven by constant relative-status competition, are essential to some people's desire for change and novelty. They never deliver permanent increases in happiness, but they aren't necessarily detrimental to utility already attained.

In the third category we might find congestion and environmental effects which mean that higher aggregate income can actually degrade aspects of quality of life.

It feels intuitively obvious that we face a mix of patterns of this sort.[16] But perfect market economics tells us that this cannot be the case if all markets are complete, all goods are traded in markets, and all individuals are rationally capable of discerning their own self-interest. In those circumstances, the curves cannot at any one time display a different curvature; if they did, consumption would be shifted from one category to another so as to make the curves exactly the same at the margin.

But we know these conditions of perfect markets and rationally self-interested individuals do not apply, for three reasons:

• Some goods are inherently public, or are most efficiently produced in a public form, so that the tradeoff between expenditures (for example, how much to spend on school sports facilities, or on attractive public spaces, or on public health care) has to be a social and political choice as well as a private one.

• People's preferences, which drive the allocation of income to alternative consumption possibilities, are not pure products of a rational satisfaction-maximizing process; rather, they are deeply influenced by social mores, by fashion, and by the deliberate efforts of marketing departments to persuade people to buy things that will not make them permanently happier, or to buy things that make them unhealthy and, as a result, less happy.

• Products and services can produce externalities—for example, my decision to drive along the road imposes a congestion penalty on others that doesn't enter into my individual decision-making process.

For these three reasons, we can have no confidence that the fruits of economic growth will be used in a way likely to foster increased life satisfaction—i.e., that we will have good growth rather than bad growth. And to some degree public policy has always recognized that fact. We make public choices that allocate some resources to inherently public amenities and goods. We try to contain environmental externalities. And the concept of "nudge" is about to enter Britain's pension policy. From 2012 on, all employees will be "nudged" to save for a pension via automatic enrollment, in recognition that people do not make rationally self-interested choices in relation to long-term savings.

The question, therefore, is not whether there is a role for public policy in achieving a better balance, but whether we already have the balance right or whether instead we need to adjust it. If the marginal-utility curves were truly shaped as in figure 3.1, an omniscient paternalist might devote more resources to the consumption categories that ensure longer life and better health, and seek to limit the more harmful side effects of poor individual choices (for instance, through restrictions or taxes on the advertising of some categories of goods). But the former might require additional taxes or nanny-state interventions, which many would resent, and the latter would restrict freedom. And we cannot be free to choose without some people making choices they subsequently regret.

Thus, I have no magic answer to the question of "good growth" versus "bad growth," only the conclusion that good economics gives us no magic answer. We have no reason to be certain that the free flow of purely individual market-driven choice, operating under the influence of social fashion and self-interested marketing, will produce the allocation of consumption expenditures that maximizes life satisfaction. And we cannot, therefore, escape the need for a continual process of political debate about whether and how we might influence the allocation in a more favorable direction.

What to do about inequality?
The second difficult issue is what, if anything, to do about inequality. The instrumental conventional wisdom has justified inequality because and to the extent that it creates incentives that help to generate faster growth, which in turn fosters happiness. But if that logic is not correct, what follows?

I don't think a definite answer is possible, and I certainly don't think economics provides us with one. Rather, I think we have to recognize that issues relating to income distribution, and to inequality, are inherently political and judgmental. In relation to these issues, economics can only point out what is not true and identify some limits within which the political debate has to proceed.

So what does economics tell us?

First, the economics of happiness, which I considered in chapter 1, tells us that relative income does matter to a significant degree—that people care about relative-status competition as well as about absolute income, and that economists interested in understanding end objectives, such as welfare or happiness, should recognize that fact rather than dismiss it as (in Martin Feldstein's words) "spiteful egalitarianism." How much inequality matters and what particular forms of inequality matter can, of course, be debated. Inequality between the bottom of the income distribution and the middle probably matters a lot: a sense of being unable to have the lifestyle enjoyed by the majority of one's fellow citizens is highly likely to be a barrier to contentment. But extreme and growing equality between the middle and the top probably matters too, though not perhaps in relation to the very top (i.e., a few billionaires whose lifestyle can be vicariously followed without any particular sense of resentment or exclusion). It is, I think, a reasonable hypothesis, as Pickett and Wilkinson are in effect arguing, that if a sufficiently large number of people move further and further away from the median income (in the UK, say, several hundred thousand people rather than simply a few thousand), the existence of such a highly visible and large income elite may have a significant effect on the intensity of status competition, and on the ability of societies to share common concerns and coalesce around collective objectives. Certainly nothing in economics excludes that possibility, and understanding it is crucial—particularly if, as I argued in chapter 1, the very process of increasing average income may tend to lead naturally to greater inequality at the top.

Second, sound economics and social science suggest that there are some apparent answers to the issue of inequality that are not convincing and/or certainly not in themselves adequate. Three insights from good economics are particularly important here:

• If inequality is important, its negative effect cannot be overcome by growth in average income alone, since growth in absolute income leaves the intensity of relative-income competition unchanged.

• "Increasing skills"—the all-purpose and all-party response to the problem—is unlikely to be sufficient. The skills argument often focuses on "skilling up" the workforce so that a larger percentage of the population can work in highly paid internationally competitive sectors. But in modern economies only a relatively small percentage of all jobs are found in internationally competitive sectors—and success in those sectors often involves capital intensity, automation, and minimal potential for the creation of new jobs. The vast majority of jobs in a rich developed economy are in non-traded sectors of the economy—retailing, wholesale distribution, leisure, health, education. Fewer than 100,000 people work for Microsoft; more than a million work for Walmart. In employment terms, "it's *not* the *e*-conomy stupid."[17] So the crucial question is this: What determines the relative pay rate of the shelf stacker in the supermarket versus the chief executive of the supermarket chain, a differential that has widened greatly over the last 30 years? We don't know for sure, but it isn't clear that higher skills for the unskilled will change such income differentials, which result from the competition in *relative* skills that determines who ends up in what job.[18]

• How about equality of opportunity—removing the unfair influences of inheritance, and equalizing access to educational and other opportunities? Well, opportunities for all are certainly desirable, but they are not a panacea, as Michael Young noted 53 years ago in *The Rise of the Meritocracy*,[19] a prescient book that deserves wider reading or re-reading today. There is nothing in Pickett and Wilkinson's analysis or in the economics of happiness to suggest that the impact on well-being of relative failure in the competition for relative status would be mitigated by knowing that the fault lay in your genes rather than in your inheritance.

So there are no easy ways to avoid the issues of inequality of outcome.

Third, although there are constraints on our ability to offset income and equality through progressive taxation, these constraints are somewhat different in nature from those that are often proposed, and not as extreme. The constraint most often mentioned is the impact on incentives. And incentives do matter even if growth will not deliver permanently increased happiness—without any incentives we would face the economic regression and stagnation of the pure planned economy. But the idea that incentives require lower tax rates for the rich—an idea that as recently as 2006 had some British commentators talking excitedly about the merits of a flat income tax—is often hugely overstated. For most of my adult life I have been lucky enough to earn an income that put me in the highest tax bracket (at first 60 percent, then 40 percent, and now 50 percent). Those variations have made no difference whatever to how hard I have worked, nor have I observed any change in the work effort of other highly paid people around me. Insofar as highly paid people are driven by income rather than by job status and professionalism per se, they are driven by *relative* income, since it is relative income that determines their ability to win in the competition for relative-status goods and positional goods (above all, pleasantly located houses), and such goods account for an increasingly large share of expenditures the richer we become. And income-tax rates paid by everyone do not change the relative-status pecking order. From an incentives point of view, the range within which variations in progressive income tax make little difference is wider than is often supposed. But other important limits are probably more important. Beyond some level, issues of international competition could become significant,[20] and beyond some level tax-avoidance activities will proliferate, both because the greater payoff from avoidance will cover the costs of ever more complex devices and because the higher the rates go the more people will feel that avoidance is fair. At 50 percent I am quite willing to pay tax as a fair contribution to a society in which I occupy a lucky position; at 80 percent I may well seek the advice of a very clever tax accountant. Each individual has his or her own sense of the limit; the aggregate combination of those limits is a sliding scale of increasingly active avoidance.

Thus, we are left with no easy definitive answers, but rather with the unavoidable issues of what is fair and what different people, operating within an economy in which they are free to choose what to consume, where to work, and what to purchase, perceive to be fair. And most people accept some inequality, and indeed significant inequality, as fair. Ask people whether they resent the high market value of high artistic or sporting talent and they tend to say No, because they can understand what skills delivered that pay. Most people also accept that jobs with high levels of responsibility should receive significantly higher pay. And most of us accept that an entrepreneur who has developed a restaurant or a restaurant chain, or a hotel, or a piece of engineering or software that delights us, should receive a high return. The deal feels fair in view of the benefits we feel we are receiving.

Other sources of income—for example, activities perceived to be entirely distributive or rent-extracting—excite resentment. But, as I discussed in chapter 1, and as Roger Bootle emphasized, economic activities are often partly distributive and partly creative, with no clear divide. Most jobs turn out to have both distributive and creative elements. Most successful entrepreneurs end up rich through a mix of creative and distributive activities. A real-estate developer who helps create attractive new urban environments typically also makes money from clever schemes to minimize tax payments and from the careful timing of purchases and sales within the asset-price cycle. And competition via distributive activities is a part of the process that ensures the success of the most efficient and innovative firms.

So there are no clear answers to the question of how progressive the taxation system should be, and there is no possibility of a tax system ever distinguishing between creative and distributive activities. Nor is there any possibility that we will ever produce an economy in which all activities are, to use Bootle's term, creative. Instead, only two limited but perhaps still important implications follow:

• We have to accept that inequality is an inherently political issue. Notions of "fairness" are bound to play some part, and the limits set by purely economic considerations do not tightly constrain the range of feasible political solutions.

• We should aim to counteract any large and obvious and powerful tendencies for the proliferation of purely distributive activities—which, as I argued in chapter 2, are particularly in danger of developing within the financial sector.

3.3   The Discipline of Economics

I began by referring to the dominant conventional wisdom that played a major role in the political discourse of the last three to four decades and had a pervasive influence on public policy. I have argued that, both as regards objectives (the maximization of measured GDP) and as regards means (free markets as the universal formula for economic efficiency and growth), the conventional wisdom is either wrong or hugely simplistic, and should be rejected.

But does that rejection also imply a rejection of important tendencies in academic economics? Was the discipline of economics at fault, or should we instead blame simplifications by non-academic users of economics and perversions by lobbying interests, absolving the discipline of economics from any blame? Robert Skidelsky argues in *The Return of the Master* that our response to the recent financial crash should involve not only changes in policy but also a reconstruction of economics itself.[21] Is that right?

The case for the prosecution of the discipline of economics would go as follows.[22]

For more than 50 years, the dominant strain of academic economics has been concerned with exploring, through complex mathematics, how economically rational human beings interact in markets. And the conclusions reached have appeared optimistic, indeed at times Panglossian. Kenneth Arrow and Gerard Debreu illustrated that a competitive market economy with a fully complete set of markets was Pareto-efficient.[23] New classical macroeconomists such as Robert Lucas argued that if human beings are not only rational in their preferences and choices but also in their expectations, then the macro economy will have a strong tendency toward equilibrium, with sustained involuntary unemployment a non-problem.

And tests of the efficient-market hypothesis appeared to illustrate that liquid financial markets are driven not by the patterns of chartist fantasy but by the efficient processing of all available information, making the actual price of a security a good estimate of its intrinsic value.

Economics therefore provided strong support for the proposition that totally free markets achieved the objective of allocative efficiency. And it also tended to assume that allocative efficiency and income growth over time were desirable objectives, and that increased income delivered increased utility, which could be equated with life satisfaction. This was in part because any deeper inquiry into the relationship between income and welfare or happiness would have interfered with mathematical precision, which required a precisely defined maximand.

Of course, as a description of academic economics this is not only a simplification but a caricature. Throughout the last 50 years, much of academic economics has been devoted quite explicitly to understanding why and under what conditions these simplistic assumptions do not apply. Kenneth Arrow himself spent much of his career exploring the market imperfections that made his demonstration of a Pareto-efficient equilibrium inapplicable in the real world. Richard Lipsey and Kelvin Lancaster illustrated that if some markets were imperfect then making other markets closer to perfect might not be welfare-optimal.[24] George Stigler and others considered the costs of gathering the information required to make markets efficient. Many researchers, including Lawrence Summers, James Poterba, and Robert Shiller, found serial correlations and other patterns in share prices, which contradicted simple efficient-market hypotheses. All economic textbooks included taxonomies of potential market failure, which might justify policy interventions such as pollution taxes and provision of public goods. And, more fundamentally, the work of James Mirrlees, Joseph Stiglitz, and George Akerlof illustrated that once we really understand the implications of information economics, markets can settle far from an efficient equilibrium, and equilibria can be multiple and fragile. Meanwhile, Daniel Kahneman and other behavioral economists questioned the very assumption of rational choice, of a *homo economicus* driven solely by the parts of his brain devoted to rational information processing. And Sen and others kept alive questions about whether we were right to assume that culmination outcomes are the sole objectives of economics, and whether these could be adequately measured by GDP.

So economics has not been monolithic; it has explored complexities and made assumptions clear, and it has produced multiple schools of thought. The most prestigious prizes have gone to people of strongly opposing views, and some of those views help us understand why the financial crisis occurred and lead us to question the conventional definition of income maximization as the overriding objective.

If there has been such diversity, do we really need, as Skidelsky argues, to "reconstruct economics"? My conclusion is that we do. Because the fact remains that, although academic economics included many strands, in the translation of ideas into ideology, and ideology into policy and business practice, one oversimplified strand dominated in the pre-crisis years, and that domination, though partly a perversion and simplification of economics, was also based on some dangerous tendencies within the dominant strand of economics itself.

Keynes famously wrote that "the ideas of economists and political philosophers, both when they are right and when they are wrong, are more powerful than commonly understood," and that "practical men, who believe themselves to be quite exempt from any intellectual influences, are usually the slaves of some defunct economist." However, I suspect that the greater danger lies not with entirely practical men or women exempt from any intellectual influence, but with reasonably intellectual men and women who are employed in the policy-making departments of central banks, regulatory bodies, and governments, and in the risk-management departments of banks, who are aware of intellectual influences, but who tend to gravitate to simplified versions of the dominant beliefs of economists who are still very much alive.

It is striking how the original insights of Arrow and Debreu—precise, mathematical, and limited in their implications by the limits of their assumptions—appeared, once simplified and shed of their complexity, to provide support for the conventional wisdom.

Three steps were required to turn the precision of Arrow and Debreu into the simplification of the conventional wisdom. That simplification was partly political, but I think we should recognize it as an almost inherent product of dominant tendencies and methodological assumptions within academic economics itself.

The first of the three simplifications was to downplay the severity of the market imperfections that prevent attainment of the Arrow-Debreu equilibrium. All economists and policy makers recognize, for instance, that financial markets are not perfect. But the dominant policy response focused on identifying and seeking to rectify the specific imperfections, such as inadequate information disclosure, that seemed to prevent the attainment of market completion and perfection. The insights of Keynes and of Frank Knight relating to the role of inherent irreducible uncertainty, the insights of Stiglitz relating to information deficiencies so deep that equilibria are inherently fragile, or the insights of Kahnemann into the part rational and part irrational nature of human mental processes were far less influential in the policy mainstream. And that reflects the tendency to gravitate to assumptions that allowed mathematical tractability—that, *pace* Robert Lucas, allowed "the construction of a mechanical artificial world populated by interacting robots."

The second simplification was to forget that the Arrow-Debreu equilibrium is merely Pareto-optimal, not socially optimal, and that social optimality might require redistribution of the end results. Here perhaps the blame lies with those who thought they were using economics, rather than with economists themselves. But it is striking how frequently the simplifications are made even by those who, one would hope, were reasonably informed about the findings of good economics. In journals of the quality of the *Financial Times* or *The Economist* one often finds phrases like "immigration is in everyone's interest" or "free trade is clearly beneficial for society." But that is very definitely not what economics tells us; it tells us that free movement of factors of production can take us closer to a Pareto-optimal equilibrium that might be able to increase everyone's disposable income *if but only if* distributional consequences were offset by required redistribution. It tells us that free trade will tend to make the economic pie bigger, but also that some people will lose while others gain.

The third simplification took us from the Arrow-Debreu illustration of a competitive equilibrium that most efficiently satisfies a given preference set at a particular time to statements such as "market liberalization will drive national competitiveness and growth, which are the objectives of economic activity." There is no logical sequitur in this progression; to proceed from one to the other, we would first have to discuss end objectives and the relationships among income, wealth, utility, and happiness. And almost all economists would justifiably absolve themselves of having suggested that growth was the end objective.[25] But I suspect that most non-economists would believe that most economists did define economic growth as the objective. And that surely reflects the tendency of the mathematics of economics to squeeze out inquiry into what the objectives should be.

I therefore end up agreeing with Robert Skidelsky that we need not only to reject the simplifications of the dominant conventional wisdom as a perversion of good economics, but also to reconstruct the way in which economics is taught and practiced in two important respects.

First, it is essential that economics deal with the real world as it is, and in particular with human beings as they actually are, and that it not simply assume the existence of a rational *Homo economicus* in order to make economic analysis more mathematically tractable.

• It must not *assume* that additional income will, even if to a marginally declining extent, increase utility or happiness; it should concern itself with the mathematically and empirically imprecise but important issues of how happiness, welfare, utility, and income are defined and related, and with the imperfect and judgmental techniques that are necessary if we are to attempt to measure possible end objectives, such as life satisfaction and happiness.

• It must not assume that people participating in financial markets make rational assessments of future probabilities of potential outcomes, but instead should seek to understand how different people actually make decisions in different circumstances, given that human brains are endowed with both ratiocinating and instinctive elements.

• It must face head on the problems of Knightian/Keynesian inherent irreducible uncertainty, recognizing that the assumption that the expectations of economic agents are distributed around the objective probability distribution of future outcomes is a philosophical category error, since no probability of future outcomes objectively exists.

Thus, economics has to deal with the world as it is, not as economists have assumed it to be, in order to make the math tractable.

But, second, economics should recognize the importance of political, philosophical, and ethical issues, to which mathematics is incapable of giving precise answers. There is no precise answer to the question "What is the optimal degree of inequality?" It is an issue of politics. And the case for the market economy, which, as Sen says, has been predominantly presented in terms of income-maximization outcomes ("culmination outcomes"), should also be considered in terms of freedom as an end in itself. As John Hicks (although himself a major figure in the development of mathematical and outcomes-oriented economics) noted, "the liberal principles of the classical 'Smithian' or 'Ricardian' economists were not, in the first phase, economic principles; they were an application to economics of principles which were thought to apply in a much wider field. The contention that economic freedom made for economic efficiency was no more than a secondary support."[26]

A major deficiency of the conventional wisdom is that it has focused increasingly and almost exclusively on this secondary support, even as increasing prosperity has made further improvements in economic efficiency less certainly important to human welfare.

Economics, therefore, needs to return to the wider focus familiar to Smith, Hume, Ricardo, and Keynes, and to treat human beings as they are, not as we wish to model them. As Skidelsky argues, this suggests that we should accept Keynes' dictum that "economics is a moral and not a natural science"—that "no part of man's nature or his institutions must be entirely outside [the economist's] regard," and the economist should be "mathematician, historian, statesman and philosopher in some degree."

What would Lionel Robbins, in whose honor the lectures on which this book is based were given, have made of this call for a wider, more behavioral, more judgmental, less mathematical, more political economics? The predominant assumption is that he wouldn't have agreed at all. "Economics deals with observable facts," Robbins wrote, "ethics with valuations and obligations. The two fields of enquiry are not on the same plane of discourse." And when Keynes argued that "economics is essentially a moral science," he started the sentence "As against Robbins."

Robbins's economics, and the philosophy of economics set out in the 1932 *Essay on the Nature and Significance of Economic Science*,[27] were indeed precise, mathematical, and somewhat politically conservative. That essay includes a direct attack on the proposition, which Richard Layard has supported in his book *Happiness*, that we can infer a case for progressive income redistribution from the existence of declining marginal utility. That proposition, Robbins asserts, "rests upon the extension of the concept of diminishing marginal utility into a field in which it is entirely illegitimate."

But Robbins's essay, with its rigorous definition of what economics (as he defined it) could and could not say, would, if more closely followed, have helped guard against the simplification of economic propositions into the instrumental conventional wisdom.

For to Robbins, the same logic that says we can't use marginal-utility curves to justify redistribution also tells us that we should be very wary of drawing any significant inferences from aggregate calculations of national income, a technique then in early stages of development. Robbins was clear that "both the concept of world money income and of national money income have strict significance only for monetary theory."[28] This is consistent with a conclusion that quarter-by-quarter or year-by-year calculations of GDP can usefully inform policy decisions aimed at stabilizing the economy, but that the assumption that a long-term increase in per capita GDP implies something for welfare or happiness ignores the numerous conventions and assumptions necessary for its calculation.

A similar logic, moreover, guarded Robbins against any assumption that propositions related to equilibrium and allocative efficiency carried any implications for whether a competitive equilibrium was in some ultimate sense a socially good result: "There is no penumbra of approbation around the theory of equilibrium. Equilibrium is just equilibrium."[29]

Robbins was also very clear that, if the science of economics was defined in the narrow sense he preferred, economists who wished their analysis to be applicable in the real world would have to be willing to engage in wider debates. "It is highly desirable that the economist who wishes that the applications of his science should be fruitful should be fully qualified in cognate disciplines and should be prepared to invoke their assistance."[30] As a result, although Robbins didn't fully agree with John Stuart Mill's assertion that "a man is not likely to be a good economist if he is nothing else," he did agree that such an economist probably wouldn't be very useful.

What Robbins was arguing for, then, was very definitely not an economics that could acquiesce in the translation from the precision of Arrow-Debreu to an unlimited faith in free markets as the means and growth maximization as the objective. On the contrary, he was arguing for an economics profoundly aware of the very narrow range of questions to which it was capable of providing answers.

Thus, the distinction between the Keynes-Skidelsky point of view and that of Robbins is less extreme then it might at first appear. Either we say, with Keynes and Skidelsky, that the economist must be "mathematician, historian, statesman and philosopher in some degree," or we say, with Robbins, that economics should be defined in a very precise and narrow sense, and should be humble about the very limited range of questions to which it can in itself give answers, recognizing that it needs to combine with other disciplines if we wish to address really important and difficult issues about social objectives and how to achieve them.

Either way, I think that leads us to Skidelsky's conclusion that we should be very wary of teaching and practicing economics as a narrowly defined discipline unconnected to others.

And either way, it says that public policy should never be based on the delusion that there is a corpus of mathematically precise economics that provides either a definition of desirable objectives or certainty as to the means by which to achieve them. We need to recognize that economic policy choices are political rather than narrowly economic in nature. "There is nothing in economics," wrote Lionel Robbins, "which relieves us of the obligation to choose."[31] Too many policy makers and politicians who at least thought they were drawing on the insights of economists forgot or chose to ignore that fact in the several decades of conventional wisdom and apparent certainty that led up to the financial crisis.

Notes

Introduction

1. Robert Skidelsky, *Keynes: The Return of the Master* (Allen Lane, 2009).

2. The essence of the argument is that the avoidance of setbacks to already attained wealth or income (e.g., via job losses, home repossessions, or income losses) is very important even if further increments of average income have uncertain capacity to make people happier, and that the avoidance of involuntary unemployment is particularly important in view of the negative effect of unemployment on people's sense of well-being and self-worth. Good macroeconomic management to ensure a reasonably stable economy over time, and to achieve recovery from recession, can therefore be immensely important even if long-term growth maximization (achieving a long-term growth rate of, say, 2.0 percent, not 1.9 percent) is not the overriding objective.

3. Lionel Robbins, *An Essay on the Nature and Significance of Economic Science* (Macmillan, 1932; reprint, Macmillan 1945).

4. Lionel Robbins, *An Essay on the Nature and Significance of Economic Science* (Macmillan, 1932; reprint, Macmillan 1945).

Chapter 1

1. Richard Layard, *Happiness: Lessons from a New Science* (Penguin, 2005).

2. The question of what meaning can be attached to measures of national income is addressed in chapter 2. Robbins commented on it perceptively in his *Essay on the Nature and Significance of Economic Science* (Macmillan, 1932; reprint: Macmillan 1945).

3. Richard A. Easterlin, "Will Raising the Incomes of All Increase the Happiness of All?" *Journal of Economic Behavior and Organization* 27 (1995): 35–47.

4. Bruno S. Frey and Alois Stutzer, *Happiness and Economics: How the Economy and Institutions Affect Human Well-Being* (Princeton University Press, 2001), 8, 77.

5. Richard Layard, *Happiness: Lessons from a New Science* (Penguin, 2005).

6. Angus Maddison, *The World Economy: A Millennial Perspective* (OECD, 2006).

7. However, Jared Diamond argues in *Guns, Germs, and Steel: The Fates of Human Societies* (Norton, 1999) that the first transformation, the development of agriculture, while enabling the creation of complex states and their elite architecture and art, may well in fact have produced an average standard of living—measured for instance by calorie intake relative to hours of work required to produce food—which was actually lower than that of hunter-gatherer societies.

8. Paul Collier, *The Bottom Billion: Why the Poorest Countries Are Failing and What Can Be Done About It* (Oxford University Press, 2007).

9. Daniel W. Sacks, Betsey Stevenson, and Justin Wolfers, Subjective Well-Being, Income, Economic Development and Growth, NBER working paper 16441, 2010).

10. See chapter 3, subsections 3.1.1 and 3.2.6. It is also worth noting that any finding of *no* cross-country correlation between life satisfaction and income when comparing rich countries would be inconsistent with the finding (on which all researchers agree) that relative income within a society matters, since the relevant measure of relative income must, to a degree, be international. Thus, for instance, the ability of British people to afford more pleasant hotels at European skiing or beach resorts is determined by income relative to that of other Europeans, and not just relative to other Britons. In addition, advertising and product promotion stimulate aspirations for a standard of living that is, to a significant degree, internationally defined. If the hypothesis is that both absolute and relative income are important, but relative income is the more important driver of happiness, then empirical evidence compatible with this hypothesis would combine strongest correlations for income variations within countries; somewhat weaker correlations for cross-country comparisons; and the weakest and most uncertain correlations and lowest gradients for long-period time series. The evidence presented by Sacks, Stevenson, and Wolfers is compatible with this hypothesis.

11. See Sacks, Stevenson, and Wolfers, "Subjective Well-Being, Income, Economic Development and Growth," figure 1.7 and discussion on page 29.

12. Lionel Robbins, "The Subject Matter of Economics," in *An Essay on the Nature and Significance of Economic Science*.

13. Robbins emphasizes the need to be very careful in applying concepts of marginal utility to issues of overall welfare, rather than simply to the determination of relative prices, arguing indeed that the application of marginal concepts to issues of human welfare maximization was simple the accidental result of the historical association of English economics with Benthamite utilitarianism. See Robbins, *Essay*, 141. Although this rigorous delineation of the limits of what economic science can contribute can be used to argue against the attempt to address the issue of objectives discussed in this chapter, it also, as I will suggest in chapter 3, helps guard against the simplistic assumption that growth and income necessarily deliver increasing aggregate happiness.

14. See note 10 above for a discussion of why relative income concerns should logically imply some correlation between satisfaction and average income when analyzed on a cross-country basis.

15. Roger Bootle, *The Trouble with Markets: Saving Capitalism from Itself* (Nicholas Brealey, 2009).

16. William Baumol, "Entrepreneurship: Productive, Unproductive and Destructive," *Journal of Business Venturing* 8, no. 3 (1990): 197–210.

17. To illustrate the complexity of the distinction, Bootle points out that even the activities of teachers, which we might assume to be entirely creative (since they either impart a direct consumption benefit of enjoyable knowledge or provide skills which are in turn used to enable "creative" activity), might in some circumstances be distributive. Thus, if one of the functions that better education plays is to signal superior skills, enabling individual A to beat individual B in the job market, but without the skills imparted being relevant to any subsequent "creative" economic activity, teaching such skills to ensure success in assessments and examinations is an essentially distributive activity. The extent to which success in the job market is driven by perceived relative skill rather than absolute skill is important to the issue of whether increasing inequality can be countered by "increasing skills." I will consider this in chapter 3.

18. The implication of the fact that activities (and in particular financial market activities) might entail a mix of the "indirectly creative" and the "distributive" has important implications for our ability to determine whether the expansion of a particular category of activity is "socially useful," and for the ability of those involved in that activity to place the pursuit of private gain within appropriate ethical bounds. This issue is perceptively considered by Raghuram Rajan in chapter 6 of *Fault Lines* (Princeton University Press, 2010). I will address it in chapter 2 (section 2.4).

19. The importance of understanding that national income accounting is the product of a set of somewhat arbitrary conventions, and the implications of this for the limited range of economic policy questions to which measures of GDP are directly relevant, was emphasized by Lionel Robbins, who wrote at a time when national income accounting was in its infancy. See Robbins, *Essay*, 57. I will return to the importance of this insight in chapter 3.

20. Andrew Haldane, Simon Brennan, and Vasileios Madouros, "What Is the Contribution of the Financial Sector: Miracle or Mirage?" in *The Future of Finance: The LSE Report 2010* (London School of Economics, 2010).

21. Sherwin Rosen explained the process by which mass communications media tended to increase the inequality of distribution of incomes of performance artists in "The Economics of Superstars," *American Economic Review* 71, no. 5 (1981): 845–858. Since then the forces identified by Rosen have intensified.

22. Robbins, *Essay*, 58.

23. In *Unjust Rewards: Exposing Greed and Inequality In Britain Today* (Granta Books, 2008), Polly Toynbee and David Walker provide a description of how many of the highest-paid gain reassurance from the belief that they *deserve* their high rewards, rather than seeing them simply as the rewards which the markets happens to allocate today because of today's specific balance of supply and demand for different skills and because of today's specific institutional structure. There really were investment bankers who felt "insulted" to be paid "only" £2 million when the trader next door was paid £4 million.

24. Tony Atkinson, "Economics as a Moral Science," Joseph Rowntree Foundation Lecture, University of York, 2008. The increase in the arithmetic mean treats equally an additional increase of income accruing to high and low income earners (since it adds all income and divides by the number of people). The increase in the geometric mean effectively treats equally an equal *percentage* increase accruing to people of different income levels.

25. Rajan, *Fault Lines*, chapter 1.

26. Kate Pickett and Richard Wilkinson, *The Spirit Level: Why More Equal Societies Almost Always Do Better* (Penguin, 2009).

27. David Cameron, "The Big Society," Hugo Young Memorial Lecture, London, 2009.

28. Charles Moore, "Inequality Is Not a Social Illness to Be 'Cured'" (review of Wilkinson and Pickett, *The Spirit Level*), *Telegraph* (UK), 9 February 2010.

29. John Kay, "The Spirit Level," *Financial Times*, 23 March 2009.

30. The ethnic homogeneity of Scandinavian countries has decreased significantly in the last few decades. But so too has support for the broad social-democratic consensus that delivered the levels of social provision and cohesion that Pickett and Wilkinson applaud.

31. This "ability to isolate" may in part be a function of population density and the potential for spatial separation. The extent to which higher-income Americans living in outer suburbs, exurbs, or gated communities can inhibit a world almost entirely disconnected from less fortunate parts of the United States is striking. This raises complex issues relating to the definition of the "community" within which people effectively live.

32. Martin Feldstein, "Rethinking Social Insurance," *American Economic Review* 95 (2005), March: 1–24.

33. This could, for instance, be among the explanations for the apparent startling difference in the relationship between economic growth and life satisfaction among the UK, Italy, and France seen in figure 1.10. Several explanations are, however, possible, and considerable further analyses would be required to confirm that the apparent difference is a real phenomenon before seeking detailed explanations for it. If it is not a real phenomenon, however, this would also cast doubt on the conclusion that the Eurobarometer results establish *any* overall relationship between income growth and life satisfaction.

34. Bruno S. Frey and Alois Stutzer, *Happiness and Economics: How the Economy and Institutions Affect Human Well-Being* (Princeton University Press, 2001), 95–110.

35. Amartya Sen, *Development as Freedom* (Oxford University Press, 1999).

Chapter 2

1. Ha-Joon Chang, *23 Things They Don't Tell You About Capitalism* (Allen Lane, 2010).

2. Carmen M. Reinhart and Kenneth S. Rogoff, *This Time Is Different: Eight Centuries of Financial Folly* (Princeton University Press, 2009).

3. Moritz Schularick and Alan M. Taylor, "Credit Booms Gone Bust: Monetary policy, Leverage Cycles and Financial Crises, 1870–2008," National Bureau of Economic Research working paper 15512, 2009 (http://www.nber.org/papers/w15512).

4. I am indebted to Jonathan Portes, until 2011 Chief Economist at the UK Cabinet Office, for sharing with me an unpublished article that provides a particularly clear description of the differences between the neoclassical and Keynes/Minsky approaches.

5. Kenneth J. Arrow and Gerard Debreu, "Existence of an Equilibrium for a Competitive Economy," *Econometrica* 22, no. 3 (1954): 265–290.

6. The quote is from Jonathan Portes's paper.

7. Richard G. Lipsey and Kelvin Lancaster, "The General Theory of the Second Best," *Review of Economic Studies* 24, no. 1 (1956–1957): 11–32.

8. John Maynard Keynes, *The General Theory of Employment, Interest and Money* (Macmillan, 1936; reprint Macmillan, 2007), chapter 12.

9. Charles MacKay, *Extraordinary Public Delusions and the Madness of Crowds* (1852; reprint: Wilder, 2008).

10. Charles Kindleberger, *Manias, Panics, and Crashes: A History of Financial Crises* (Basic Books, 1978; revised and enlarged, 1989; third edition 1996).

11. Robert J. Shiller, *Irrational Exuberance*, second edition. (Princeton University Press 2005). See also *Market Volatility* (MIT Press, 1992).

12. Hyman P. Minsky, *Stabilizing an Unstable Economy* (Yale University Press 1986).

13. Andrew Haldane, "Patience and Finance" (paper, Oxford China Business Forum, Beijing, 9 September 2010).

14. George Akerlof and Robert Shiller, *Animal Spirits: How Human Psychology Drives the Economy, and Why It Matters for Global Capitalism* (Princeton University Press, 2009).

15. Joseph E. Stiglitz, "Information and the Change in the Paradigm of Economics" (Nobel Prize Lecture, Stockholm University, 2001).

16. Roman Frydman and Michael D. Goldberg, *Beyond Mechanical Markets: Asset Price Swings, Risk, and the Role of the State* (Princeton University Press, 2011).

17. Frank Knight, *Risk, Uncertainty and Profit* (Hart, Schaffner & Marx, 1921).

18. John Maynard Keynes, *A Treatise on Probability* (Macmillan, 1920).

19. Mervyn King, "Uncertainty in Macroeconomic Policy Making—Art or Science?" Presented at Royal Society Conference on Handling Uncertainty in Science, London, 2010.

20. Stanley Fischer, "Capital-Account Liberalization and the Role of the IMF," in *Should the IMF Pursue Capital-Account Convertibility?* (Essays in International Finance No. 207, Princeton University, 1998).

21. "Capital Flows and Emerging Market Economies" (paper 33, Committee on the Global Financial System, 2009).

22. Dani Rodrik and Arvind Subramanian, "Why Did Financial Liberalisation Disappoint?" (http://www.iie.com/publications/papers/subramanian0308.pdf), 2008.

23. Jagdish Bhagwati, "The Capital Myth: The Difference between Trade in Widgets and Dollars," *Foreign Affairs* 77, no. 3 (1998): 77–85.

24. Barry Eichengreen, *Globalizing Capital: A History of the International Monetary System*, second edition (Princeton University Press, 2008), 49–55.

25. In addition to earlier references, see George Soros, *The New Paradigm for Financial Markets: The Credit Crisis of 2008 and What It Means* (Public Affairs, 2008).

26. For a discussion of this argument, see Richard Cooper, "Should Capital-Account Convertibility Be a World Objective?" in *Should the IMF Pursue Capital-Account Convertibility?* (Essays in International Finance 207, Princeton University, 1998).

27. See e.g., Raghuram Rajan, "Has Financial Development Made the World Riskier?" (lecture, Kansas City Federal Reserve Annual Economic Policy Symposium, Jackson Hole, 2005).

28. Benjamin Friedman, "Overmighty Finance Levies a Tithe on Growth," *Financial Times*, 26 August 2009 (http://www.ft.com/).

29. Dimitri Vayanos and Paul Woolley, "An Institutional Theory of Movement and Reversal," discussion paper 621, Paul Woolley Centre, London School of Economics, 2009.

30. Walter Bagehot, "Introductory," in *Lombard Street: A Description of the Money Market* (Henry S. King, 1873; reprint, fourteenth edition, 1915).

31. Robert G. King and Ross Levine, "Finance and Growth: Schumpeter Might Be Right," *Quarterly Journal of Economics* 108, no. 3 (1993): 717–737. See also Peter L. Rousseau and Richard Sylla, "Emerging Financial Markets and Early U.S. Growth," National Bureau of Economic Research working paper 7448, 1999.

32. Raghuram Ragan, *Fault Lines: How Hidden Fractures Still Threaten the World Economy* (Princeton University Press, 2010).

33. The availability of credit can enhance welfare directly through the increased choice it allows people rather than because it directly increases growth. Indeed, wider credit availability in China could slow GDP growth (through reducing the savings rate) but would allow people more choice on the timing of consumption and would allow more income to flow through to increased consumption and human well-being.

34. Robert Lucas, *Professional Memoir*, 2001, p. 21, quoted in Roman Frydman and Michael D. Goldberg, *Beyond Mechanical Markets: Asset Price Swings, Risk, and the Role of the State* (Princeton University Press, 2011).

Chapter 3

1. John Maynard Keynes, "Concluding Notes on the Social Philosophy Towards Which the General Theory Might Lead," in *The General Theory of Employment, Interest and Money* (Macmillan, 1936; reprint Macmillan, 2007), chapter XXIV.

2. Amartya Sen, "The Perspective of Freedom," in *Development as Freedom* (Oxford University Press, 1999), 13.

3. Sen makes the point in "The ends and means of development," in *Development as Freedom* (p. 35).

4. Though the potential benefit of improved allocative efficiency (or of a higher savings rate) is often loosely described as "increased growth," it should more formally be described as a transitional increase in the growth rate followed by a permanent steady-state path of income higher than would otherwise pertain. The term "medium-term growth rate" is therefore used to refer to this transitional effect.

5. See Basel Committee on Banking Supervision, "An Assessment of the Long-Term Impact of Stronger Capital and Liquidity Requirements" (Bank of International Settlements, August 2010, http://www.bis.org/publ/bcbs173.pdf); Macro Economic Assessment Group, "Assessing the Macroeconomic Impact of the Transition to Stronger Capital and Liquidity Requirements" (Bank for International Settlements, December 2010, http://www.bis.org/publ/othp12.pdf); Macro Economic Assessment (MAG), Long Term Economic Impact study (LEI) and FSA, etc., etc.

6. The analysis suggests that the impact on the growth rate is transitional, but with a transitionally lower growth rate producing a permanently slightly lower long-term steady-state path of GDP.

7. Lionel Robbins, *An Essay on the Nature and Significance of Economic Science* (Macmillan, 1932; reprint, Macmillan, 1945), 57. Robbins indeed argued that even in principle the use of GDP or per capita GDP figures to make inferences relating to aggregate or average utility was methodologically flawed: "The addition of prices or individual incomes to form social aggregates is an operation with very little meaning. . . . As expressions of an order of preference, a relative scale, they are incapable of addition. Their aggregate has no meaning. They are only significant in relation to each other. Estimates of the social income may have a quite definitive meaning for monetary theory, but beyond this they have only *conventional* significance."

8. Nicholas Stern, *The Economics of Climate Change: The Stern Review* (Cambridge University Press, 2006).

9. For a criticism of Stern's choice of discount rate, see William Nordhaus, "An Alternative Perspective: The Stern Review," in *A Question of Balance: Weighing the Options on Global Warming Policies* (Yale University Press, 2008), 165.

10. The crucial theoretical issues here are whether it is possible meaningfully to aggregate different categories of utility (e.g., the utility I gain from buying a bigger car and the utility from beautiful countryside), whether one can always trade off additional units of category A utility versus category B utility, and whether one can assume that money prices (or heroic attempts to infer what money prices would be for unpriced goods) capture the terms of this aggregate tradeoff. This issue is considered in the subsection on good and bad growth.

11. Estimated benefits of reduced journey times are often only accurate in the period before additional induced traffic produces congestion externalities. But in principle, developments could have benefits as well as disadvantages.

12. Bruno S. Frey and Alois Stutzer, "Constitution: Popular Referenda and Federalism" and "Outcome and Process," in *Happiness and Economics: How the Economy and Institutions Affect Human Well-Being* (Princeton University Press, 2001), 133, 153.

13. For a more detailed rebuttal of the argument that population stabilization and an aging population create severe economic problems and require a demographic (immigration or birth rate) response, see Adair Turner, "Do We Need More Immigrants or Babies?" (lecture presented at London School of Economics, 28 November 2007), reprinted as "Population Priorities: The Challenge of Continued Rapid Population Growth" in *Philosophical Transactions of the Royal Society B* 364, 2009: 2977–29984.

14. Of course, an argument for a focus on aggregate nominal GDP can be based not on the belief that this increases human contentment but on the belief that relative national geopolitical and military power are important to the avoidance of negative setbacks to income and life satisfaction. For an argument that Europe is deluding itself if it believes that it can concentrate on what gives Europeans life satisfaction rather than on military power relative to other nations, see Robert Kagan, *Paradise and Power: America and Europe in the New World Order* (Atlantic Books, 2003). The argument that any one country needs to maintain population growth in order to increase status and power relative to others is clearly not likely to produce an attractive global result.

15. Richard Layard, "Can We Afford to Be Secure?" and "Can Mind Control Mood?" in *Happiness: Lessons from a New Science* (Penguin, 2005), 167, 187.

16. If the reality is that we face a variety of impacts of economic growth—some positive and some negative—the aggregate relationship between income growth and human well-being for any one country might be either flat, increasing slightly or declining slightly, depending on the balance of the three factors at work. The empirical evidence for rich developed countries considered in chapter 1 (e.g., figures 1.1–1.8) is compatible with the possibility that different countries have achieved different degrees of success in the translation of rising income into rising contentment.

17. The phrase "It's not the e-conomy, stupid" was used by Tony Blair's government in the late 1990s. See Adair Turner, "It's Not the E-conomy, Stupid," in *Just Capital: The Liberal Economy* (Macmillan, 2001).

18. Skill enhancement might narrow this differential, but through a mechanism different from that often described. Rather than the skill enhancement producing a "better more productive shelf stacker," if shelf stackers were trained to a higher level in generic skills potentially applicable to some other higher-paid job, this might reduce the pay differential between shelf stacking and the slightly higher-paid job. This would be because the differential would be limited by the potential for companies to employ an adequate alternative for the higher-skill job, rather than pay a higher differential to those best able to perform it. Differentials could thus be reduced not by ensuring that everyone has a "high-skilled high-paid job" (the standard political statement) but by ensuring that those in lower-skill jobs have sufficient skills that they could adequately perform jobs for which they are not in fact selected (given the presence of people with still higher skills) and thus are at least relevant to equilibrium market prices for such jobs. How far this effect operates in a world where skills are not just learned initially, but systematically refined and developed by doing, is, however, not clear. Thus, while increasing skills to ensure that people have as many chances as possible is for many reasons undoubtedly desirable, we cannot be certain that it will in itself significantly ameliorate increasing inequality.

19. Michael Young, *The Rise of the Meritocracy 1870–2033: An Essay On Education and Equality* (Penguin, 1958).

20. This is so in part because, while what matters to high-income people is relative rather than absolute income, the international relativity may be important: one's ability to afford a pleasant foreign holiday, or to own a house abroad, depends on income relative to others in other countries, not solely within the domestic economy.

21. See Robert Skidelsky, "Keynes for Today," in *Keynes: The Return of the Master* (Allen Lane, 2009), 168.

22. For a summary of the prosecution case, see Skidelsky, "Keynes for Today"; also see John Cassidy, *How Markets Fail* (Allen Lane, 2009).

23. Kenneth Arrow and Gerard Debreu, "Existence of Equilibrium for a Competitive Economy," *Econometrica* 22 (1954): 265–290.

24. Richard Lipsey and Kelvin Lancaster, "The General Theory of the Second Best," *Review of Economic Studies* 24, no. 1 (1956–1957): 11–32.

25. At very least, all economists, even if willing to assume that further increments of money income must convert into additional aggregate utility, recognize a tradeoff that individuals make between additional leisure and additional income. As a result, though some professional economists might be willing to define the maximization of GDP per hour worked as a reasonable end objective, none should be willing to support making maximization of per capita GDP the explicit objective except when hedged round with suitable reservations. In the translation to "practical men" economics, however, it is per capita GDP (or even aggregate national GDP) that tends to be assumed as the end objective.

26. John Richard Hicks, *Wealth and Welfare*, volume 1 of *Collected Essays in Economic Theory* (Blackwell, 1981), 138.

27. Lionel Robbins, *An Essay on the Nature and Significance of Economic Science* (Macmillan, 1932; reprint, Macmillan, 1945), 137.

28. Ibid., 57.

29. Ibid., 131.

30. Ibid., 150.

31. Ibid., 152.

Index